THE LYCIA

C000120847

The Lycian Shore is an accoun... Minor coast of Turkey, follow... and Persians, and the men who prepared the scene for Alexander the Great. Just as the ancient voyagers did, they landed as the tides and winds allowed.

It was no ordinary journey, but an adventure into the past. Freya Stark's knowledge and descriptive powers make this an imaginative guide to a past civilization and way of life. Her intention is to 'fill out the meaning of space with something of its substance in time. Every bay or headland of these shores ... carries visible and invisible signs of its past.'

In common with *Ionia*, Freya Stark uses particular sites or areas as the basis for an appropriate theme: Chios and the fall of Athens; Island Pirates and adventure; Caunus and Alexander's Road; Aperlae and Loyalty and the Mercenaries; the Chelidonian Cape magic. No better guide could be found for the popular western coasts of Turkey.

Dame Freya Stark has become a legend in her lifetime through her travels and her ability to describe them. Born in Paris, her passion for travel was inculcated at a young age: at the age of five she could speak three languages. Educated privately in Italy, she later attended Bedford College and the School of Oriental Studies in London. She has become renowned for her accounts of travel in desert and classical regions in particular. Amongst her books are *Alexander's Path*, *Beyond the Euphrates*, *The Coast of Incense*, *Dust in the Lion's Paw*, *East is West*, *Perseus in the Wind*, and *The Southern Gates of Arabia*.

FREYA STARK

THE LYCIAN
SHORE

CENTURY
LONDON SYDNEY AUCKLAND JOHANNESBURG

NOTE

The Latin variant has been used for all classical names with the exception of some few outside Turkey. For Turkish place names English phonetic spelling has been used.

First published in 1956 by John Murray (Publishers) Ltd

This edition first published in 1989 by Century,
an imprint of Century Hutchinson Ltd, Brookmount House,
62–65 Chandos Place, Covent Garden, London WC2N 4NW

Century Hutchinson Australia Pty Ltd, 89–91 Albion Street,
Surry Hills, Sydney, New South Wales, Australia

Century Hutchinson New Zealand Limited, PO Box 40–086,
Glenfield, Auckland 10, New Zealand

Century Hutchinson South Africa (Pty) Ltd, PO Box 337,
Bergvlei, 2012 South Africa

The cover shows a painting by Edward Lear

British Library Cataloguing in Publication Data

Stark, Freya, *1893*–
    The Lycian shore.—(The Century travellers)
    1. Turkey. Lycia. Description & travel
    I. Title
    915.64

    ISBN 0–7126–2442–2

Printed by The Guerney Press, Channel Islands

CONTENTS

To 'Elfin' and her owners
this book is gratefully inscribed

I would like to thank Mr. John Sparrow, Professor A. Andrewes and Mr. John Grey Murray for their kind help and encouragement.

THE LYCIAN SHORE

Founder and harbour-god, do thou . . . send . . . the outward-bound sail down smooth water to the open sea; and . . . guard the voyager for the Pythian shrine; and . . . if all we singers are in Phoebus' care, I will sail cheerily with a fair-flowing wind.

ANTIPHELLUS, The Greek Anthology

*O heart of insatiable longing,
What spell, what enchantment allures thee
Over the rim of the world
With the sails of the sea-going ships?*

Bliss Carman's SAPPHO

1

THE VOYAGE OF *ELFIN*

For in learning these objects it is necessary at the same time to learn both what is false and what is true of the whole of existence.   PLATO, Epistle VII.

ONE OF MY FRIENDS ONCE TRIED TO TEACH PUNCTUALITY to an Arab ruler. He did it by arriving early for his appointments, and waiting in his car at the gate, watch in hand, till the actual moment struck. He apparently succeeded, but whether such a minor virtue was worth the effort has never been ascertained, and the ruler with his punctuality is dead. I think of him as I write this book, which lays no claim to any such precision and was to have been merely the straightforward tale of a journey, made in 1952 from the gulf of Smyrna round the south-west corner of Asia Minor, with David Balfour in his motor-sail-boat *Elfin*.

I was then reading the history of Alexander. He is nearly always thought of against a background of either Greece or the farther East to which his conquests led him. But it would be good, I thought, to follow him in that first adventure among the great cities of his own past on the Asiatic coast; I became anxious to learn something of the climate of that age—to study the 4th century history with a slant in the direction of Asia Minor. I wanted to discover what Alexander found in men's minds when he marched down from the Granicus in 334 B.C.

To fit such a picture into the incidents of present travel is no easy matter, and demands as it were the plaiting of a double strand. It has its advantage, since the landscape of today still fits most yesterdays in this part of the world—although it may not do so for much longer. Nor did I mean to keep very precisely within the limits of my time. I took what I found to my purpose here and there—considering the life of the pirate, for instance, as generally permanent in character, so that later and early information may be almost equally helpful while the landscapes and winds and waters on which it is based remain the same. Nor did I hold the early Hellenistic age beyond the time-limit of my subject, since it was built by the young men who travelled with Alexander and survived him. It was a product of the world as they found it and of the new ingredients they brought, so that to look at it was no more than a short glance ahead on my path—legitimate and useful in all journeys. But the Roman Empire, and Byzantium, and the Crusaders and the great Muslim eras were beyond my prospect.

Yet one is led astray; for how can one neglect a Roman gateway because it is outside one's period, or pass by St. Paul without a word because he travels in a century different from one's own? And then there is the problem of Time, its essence and its limitations.

In our age, when even Cinerama can seem to reproduce physical features of the known lands, the art of words may well attempt a rather deeper penetration and—in travel books particularly—fill out the meaning of space with something of its substance in time. In Turkey particularly, and in all the Levant and the Aegean, a journey without history is like the portrait of an old face without its wrinkles. Every bay or headland of these shores, every mountain-top round whose classic name the legends and clouds are floating, carries visible or invisible signs of its past. The spell of these landscapes is that their names and their stories are familiar, though many of the sites have been forgotten, so that one wanders as if through an inherited estate, discovering it anew.

Who would not be enamoured of Time while he lingers beside us? He is, if one comes to think of it, the closest of all our mortal companions. In his lifelong friendship—capricious, elusive, frightening, delightful—we can remember our youth

4

The mirror of History

together and need look forward to no separation except that of death. On the Asiatic shore, among so many ruined empires, he is present in the most intimate and majestic way. He was there, among the cross-currents of the 4th century, leading me to stray away from the questions I was pondering—the events of a world on whose threshold the young conqueror was about to appear—into far abstract avenues of thought.

Yet there are boundaries, and I hope that by the end of this book, having started with the fall of Athens and travelled through Lycia to the verge of Alexander the Great, I may have drawn a picture—not statistical, but animated and vague as if it were our own life—of this coast as the conqueror and his companions found it—controversial and legendary, with its remote memories and its immediate past, tangled into the endless implications of their present. For the whole of its past is present in any historical moment, and a line between the two is as arbitrary as a line between a particular wave and its sea.

The conclusions are mine, for better or worse, though others have doubtless thought of them before me. I am perhaps like a friend who was pleased to have discovered *terza rima* for himself, and I do not apologize for venturing. The past holds our future, and what is more natural than to try, when one's own door is locked, to turn the key?

'There are many things that hinder us from knowing; there is the obscurity of the subject and the shortness of human life'; and if we are wrong, we are probably not so much more wrong than those who know better. 'Availing myself of history as of a mirror, from which I learn to adjust and regulate my conduct,'[1] says Plutarch: and I think there are too few people in our age who choose to use their own wits in an honest endeavour and, with the facts in a tangle before them, sort them out into a pattern of their own.

This book therefore lays no claim to learning, but roams through space and time as books of travel should do, and its chief living personage is the *Elfin*, an easy little London-built boat of five tons. She was the first of her kind, I rather think, to have followed our route for mere pleasure, though the coast had been charted and written about in 1818 by Captain Beaufort, and was known to travellers and used by our own and other navies during the war.

D. B. sailed her round from Smyrna, and his wife Louise and I met them at Cheshme, south of the southern arm of the bay. An intensive hour or two of packing followed, interspersed with Turkish formalities and papers. Tins of food, in a basket under the table; pillows and blankets, on the seats where one slept at night or ate by day; charts, in what appeared to be the only safely dry spot—since D. B., striding in and out with a glance at my small preparations, kept on demolishing the other spots I chose. "I wouldn't put it there; it'll get wet." The floor, which the landsman thinks of as secure, was, it appeared, the most unsafe of all; I began to realize that until one has had one's two feet off the ground one has never really travelled at all.

D. B. and Louise drove home to Smyrna overland for the night and left me with the skipper and the cook, Hüseyin and Mehmet, anchored at the fork of the two Cheshme promontories. In the bottom of the bay, a Genoese castle wall showed dimly—a sloping rectangle with battlemented curtain and towers. A minaret, built later half-way down the outer wall, lifted itself clear against the sky.

The few hundred yards that separated me from the small, electrically illuminated but deserted quay, seemed to hold a remoteness of infinite travel. This magic bewitched me through all my voyage, and has thrown its light on my recollections, so that the mobilities of space and sea and time have fused, as if in a dimension of their own. Sometimes this vagueness came so near me that I would scarcely know in what age or world I travelled. As I bent over the side of

6

Time

Elfin on that first evening of late September, looking down into the night-deep water—its solid darkness and deceptive lights—the star reflections so faintly tremulous, the beams of the quay-side lamps distorted and strong and broken with every breath of air—I felt as if I too, and all of us, and Alexander, were still floating, like *Elfin*, on Time that laps us gently and waits to cover us when we drown; and spreads oblivion and beauty over the crumbled records on Aegean shores; and gives us now and then these nights, quiet and exquisite, in harbour.

2

CHIOS

The Defeat of Athens

There is a great deal of ruin in a nation. ARISTOTLE.

For of the gods we believe, and of men we know, that by a law of their nature
wherever they can rule they will. This law was not made by us . . . we did but
inherit it, and shall bequeath it to all time, and we know that you and all man-
kind, if you were as strong as we are, would do as we do.
The Athenians to the Melians. Thuc. V. 105, Jowett's translation.

THERE IS A DESCRIPTION OF CHIOS UNDER TURKISH RULE
published by Bernard Randolph in 1687. 'The inhabitants,' he says, 'enjoy greater privileges than any Greeks
in the Grand Signior's dominions . . . In the summer time
every evening the marine is full with all sorts of people with
musick, singing and dancing, and none offer to molest them.'
They had a castle; and houses well built, with 'windows red
and green'; their mole and lighthouse were ruined, so that the
harbour was dangerous in stormy weather; but the Genoese
churches were still in good repair. When the Vizier on his
return from Candy tarried several days, he was told that the
church bells he heard were bells of mules. He replied that his
informer was 'an asse for endeavouring to make me believe
so. This is some bell to call you to prayers, and be not
ashamed to enjoy the freedom that is given you'; and he went
on to ask why there were no women out of doors. Being
told that the Elders had shut them away for fear of disorder,
he had them all out again, and remarked that the Chians
should enjoy their privileges while he was there, otherwise
he would recall the liberty they had. Next morning the streets
were full with all sorts, and the singing and dancing returned.

8

The Harbour

A very long history led up to this summer pleasure, from the day when Poseidon first dallied with two nymphs on the empty island, and their sons were said to have peopled it; and then the Carians and the Cretans came.[1] Lycurgus met Homer here;[2] and Alexander the Great sent a letter carved on a block of grey marble, still to be seen. The Chian prosperity grew as it went down the ages. 'Whichever side they support,' says Isocrates, 'has proved stronger on the sea.' It was a granary for the Romans,[3] where Herod of Judaea, on his way to visit Agrippa, paid for a new portico while detained by contrary winds[4] —for it was the main north and south route of the eastern Aegean.

The Genoese came in 1346, and having taken the citadel after a three months' siege established a trading company whose name—Mahona—comes from the Arabic *ma'un* used for associations at that time.[5] The Venetians in turn besieged the Chians, and the Ottomans taxed them: but the *mastic* that grows wild on their hills stood high in the market, and the islanders and the Genoese—unhelped by their parent city—paid increasing tributes and held on. In 1471 the Venetians sacked the mainland port of Passaggio (probably Cheshme), and found an enormous booty; and then the Turkish fleet appeared, in 1566 at Easter, and the Chians continued to pay 'double what any other island in the archipelago pays',[6] till the time of the Greek war of 1912.

The town sits snugly round a comfortable harbour. Its castle and windmills crumble over the old streets while modern civic pride now goes in for schools and museums higher up the hill. Its gaiety, spread over poverty as thinly as sunlight on deep water, remains. The loungers on the quay welcomed us as we touched the island, catching the hawsers of *Elfin*, seizing our packages, helping us over the narrow crack of water, so lightly overstepped, that separates the stationary from the mobile world. A similar courtesy is shown in Turkish harbours,

but it is more detached, a general helpfulness to strangers.
To the Greek, the boat that lands is a thing that comes and
goes and never leaves one's life entirely the same. It is illuminated by the hopes and fears of all his past: for it has carried
his destiny for ages.

So the Greek islander looks at boats, with his history behind
him; and so he welcomed us in our *Elfin* when we sailed
from Cheshme across a lively sea. And when we had strolled
about, and had washed down our red mullet with *mastic*, and
sat watching the people at the café with our friends; and when
they had left for their homes in the upper vineyards, and the
roads had emptied and darkened, and *Elfin* lay moored in an
unfamiliar combination of privacy and publicity under a
street lamp against the quay, looking very small for she is
only thirty-three feet from end to end, I began to think of
this cheerfulness, that rings like a tune through all the Greek
invasions, and never flourishes very far inland, in the continents
of Africa or Asia, or even in Laconia shut in by hills. I began
to think too of what had happened in and around this harbour
—of the fighting years when Chios possessed a naval force,
and aspired to the sovereignty of the sea, and liberty[7]; and of
all the men who commanded their ships in these waters: of
Chabrias, the Athenian admiral, for instance, who died
here of wounds, in 357 B.C., worsted in a ramming attack,
while the men on the other ships of his fleet withdrew;
and of the trampling on the decks, and the shouting, and
the sweep of the oars in the water as they grew fainter in his
ears.[8]

He lived easily, was of good family, kept a racing stable,
and had commanded honourably by sea and land, in Greece
and Thrace, Egypt and Cyprus. From his fighting on the
Nile, he brought back new defence methods of trenches and
palisades, tried out in the plains of Thebes against the Spartan
king. In 376 B.C. he gained a vital sea-victory for Athens,

on the route of the grain-fleets from the Hellespont—and might have destroyed the Spartan fleet entirely if, fearful of questions in Parliament, he had not lingered to collect the shipwrecked and the dead. How little we know about these old commanders! A divergence with his former enemy Agesilaus of Sparta, when Chabrias remained faithful to the Egyptian King whom the other deserted; some advice on the raising of money (an essential art for a professional Greek general to know); and a day in the Theban war, when his men by their discipline averted the Spartan charge. He made them kneel on the rise they held, with spears uplifted and bodies unprotected, the shield unused and leaning on the ground: and King Agesilaus, seeing them so motionless and silent, so ready and so contemptuous, withdrew. Chabrias chose this pose of his men in the battle as the one by which he wished to be remembered when they voted him a statue in Athens, and twenty years later, dying in Chios harbour, he may have thought of that day; for he lived in the Aegean tradition, in small cities in sight of his friends, taking death and life with passionate acceptance:

> If I must die,
> I will encounter darkness like a bride,
> And hug it in mine arms, [9]

and 'While we all possess bodies that are mortal,' says Isocrates, 'we yet partake of immortality by virtue of good will and praise and good report and memory which keeps pace with the passage of time—a boon for which we may all strive with all our might and suffer any hardship whatsoever'.

Such heartfelt zest for public honour is alien to us, who consider it a private matter between our conscience and ourselves: yet I believe that nearly all our troubles with the Mediterranean in general come from the neglect of this ancient peculiarity —a fervour for reputation which Isocrates describes when he says that no man is by nature either democrat or oligarch but that all desire, in each case, that form of government in which they are held in honour.

Why should this count no longer in lands where so little else has changed? In the harbour where the *Elfin* was rocking gently, I began to think of boats that had come and gone— sailors serving their time, but with the same life always—a succession of brown arms with nervous fingers of seamen tying up craft of all sorts into a distance of generations innumerable.

There too, in that distance, the mistakes of today were made by the imperial powers.

Athens, in her day, made the people of Chios demolish their new walls—and eleven years later, when the Athenian Empire lay wasting in the Syracusan quarries, the humiliation was remembered, as it always is remembered. The Chians were the first to desert. They went to Sparta, together with an ambassador from Tissaphernes, the commander for King Darius in south-west Asia, and invited the Peloponnesians to come over, and promised to maintain their army. And the last battles of the Peloponnesian war were fought in these waters or around the Hellespont, during eight more years.

Her Spartan enemy, her disaffected allies, and Persia behind them, were arrayed against Athens at that time. Rejecting offers of peace, she reinstated Alcibiades as her general and— when the battle of Notium was lost in his absence—dismissed him: and yet, in spite of all, regained the mastery of the sea.

I thought of Conon, another excellent commander, sent out with nine other generals to replace Alcibiades. He found his fleet so impaired and depleted, that he could only put to sea with seventy ships, and got himself shut up in Mitylene.

The Persians were now paying the Spartan navy; a new young admiral had come out; and the odds were against Athens in the Aegean. Conon was soon blockaded in Mitylene, both by land, with an army from Chios, and by sea, and was unable to procure provisions from anywhere. The people in the city were many, and there was no way open by which he could send news of his plight to Athens. He manned two of his fastest ships inside the harbour before daybreak, picking out the best oarsmen, and setting up the side screens to hide the decks. When the enemy had become accustomed to the sight of them in port, on the fifth day, when it came to be midday and the blockaders were careless and some of them asleep, they rowed out, and one of the ships set sail for the Hellespont and the other to the open sea. The blockaders, as they severally got their ships clear of one another, cutting away their anchors and rousing themselves from sleep, pursued the vessel which had made for the open sea, and at sunset over-hauled and captured her in battle, took her in tow and brought her back, men and all, to their fleet. But the ship which had fled towards the Hellespont escaped, and on its arrival at Athens reported the blockade.

Now in this desperate crisis the whole of Athens went on board whatever ships there were. 'They voted to go to the rescue with one hundred and ten ships, putting aboard all who were of military age, whether slave or free. Even the knights went aboard in considerable numbers.' And within thirty days they sailed to Samos and collected more ships, making their number one hundred and fifty, and met the Spartans at the Arginusae islands, that lie between Lesbos and Cyme and the mainland of Asia. The weather was unsettled and it was August, which is stormy in the Aegean, and rain postponed a night attack on the Spartan side; but Callicratides, the new

young Spartan admiral, set out at daybreak, and the eight
Athenian generals stood to meet him with their ships arranged
in overlapping lines one behind the other, for their sailors
were not as skilful as the Rhodian and Chian crews who
stood against them in a single line with a view to breaking
through.

The Spartan general died, as the omens had foretold, holding
out for a long time and worn down by numbers; and the
Athenian generals won the greatest sea-battle on record of
Greek against Greek to that day. But they were too many in
command; and they rowed back to their anchorage without
first picking up their shipwrecked comrades or their dead:
they did not think in time of the August weather, which
worsened with the afternoon and kept them to the lee of the
islands; and the shipwrecked were drowned and the whole
coast of the Cymaeans and Phocaeans was strewn with corpses
and wreckage; and the Spartans blockading Mitylene escaped
to Chios, where they still counted one hundred ships. Conon,
who had been out of all this, was left; but six of the generals
who returned to Athens were condemned to death for the
neglect of their men, with no fair trial, fulfilling the dream
that one of them had dreamed before the battle. Pericles, the
son of Pericles and Aspasia, was among them; and Socrates
cast a vote in their favour.

So the second act closed in the downfall of Athens in
Asia.

At this late hour a chance for safety was given and the
Spartans asked for peace. They were tired of their Persian
subservience and offered fair terms—to clear out of Attica and
for each side to keep the cities that they held. And Athens,
unable—as I take it—after three generations of riches to face
the loss of the Ionian seaboard, rejected them. One must
remember how great the riches in question were. Forty-three
years later, when his western lands revolted, the Persian King

was deprived of 'half his revenues; and what remained were insufficient for his war'.[10]   Rather than liquidate their empire, the Athenians decided to fight on.

Five new generals, and Conon, the only first-rate captain now among them, camped at Aegospotami on the Hellespont, with all the fleet that Athens had—one hundred and eighty ships.   Alcibiades, from his castle in Thrace looked down and saw them moored on an open shore with no city nearby, and rode to advise them to shift their anchorage to Sestus. "For if you are there," he said, "you will be able to fight when you please."

The generals were not inclined to listen to a man out of office; and on the fifth day, when they were disembarked and scattered, Lysander the Spartan in Lampsacus, with the town and good harbour behind him, gave the signal to his fleet to sail. Conon alone saw the attack coming, and signalled the Athenians to haste with all their might to their ships.   Some had but two banks of oars manned, and some one, and some were entirely empty; Conon's own and seven others accompanying him, which were fully manned, put to sea in close order, and the *Paralus* (the state trireme) with them, but all the rest Lysander captured on the beach—one hundred and sixty triremes, and most of their crews he gathered up on the shore. Three thousand Athenian captives were condemned to die, with Philocles their general, who had once voted for the cutting off of the right hands of prisoners to prevent their ever again holding an oar.   Lysander asked him what he thought he deserved who had given such cruel advice against Greeks; but he was told to 'proceed as he would have been proceeded with had he been conquered', and Philocles having bathed and dressed himself in a rich robe, led his countrymen to execution.

But Conon sent the *Paralus* to Athens and she arrived at night with tidings of the disaster.   'And a sound of wailing ran from Piraeus along the long walls to the city, one man passing on the news to another; and during that night no one slept, all mourning, not for the lost alone, but far more for their own selves, thinking that they would suffer such treatment as they had visited upon the Melians . . . and many other Greek peoples . . . and it was resolved to block up all the harbours except one . . . and to get the city ready for a siege.'

So the Peloponnesian war, and the Athenian Empire overseas, came to an end. And the Greek cities of Asia and the islands, which—living perhaps under easier conditions—seem to have had no such passion for suicide as the homeland, began to learn sadly that one Greek domination was as bad as another. Chios, up to 412 B.C., had remained uninjured ever since the Persian wars. It had more slaves than any other Greek city except Sparta; and sixty triremes at the beginning of these troubles. Now it had suffered famine and siege and spoliation from Athens for seven years; and saw Lysander take the triremes from its docks; and gave pay and work on its estates to the starving and dangerous Spartan sailors. There can have been little longing for anything but peace in the islands and the coastlands when the news of the Athenian downfall travelled south.

I could not help thinking of these things in Chios harbour, where tidings must have been awaited hour by hour, dropped by the coasting caïques of that day. Now, in the very early morning, a soft hum of engines told me that their descendants, the fishing-boats around us, were preparing for the sea. We too slipped out at daybreak, and coasted down the narrows.

But we met the south-east wind as the morning brightened, and it made us put in for protection behind a nameless little headland of the southern Cheshme promontory, where a miniature bay lay sheltered and clear as glass, pale green in the climbing sun.

Past and Present

Here we spent the day in idleness. The low cliff of yellow shale with its scrub of thyme and cistus was enough to hold away the wind. The water as we swam about in it was still and immaterial, so that nothing but space seemed to divide us from the sea-urchins: self-contained in black velvet bristles, they sat scattered like Cyclades or Sporades on the untroubled sand. They appeared, I thought as I floated above them, to have mastered the art of being purely defensive—a thing that was never possible to the Athenians.

Outside our bay but quite near, the ruffle of the wind continued. One could see but not hear it making a noise, running its fingers through the blue and tangling it in waves. Safe in shelter, the *Elfin* gave a tiny movement now and then, of patience, like a sigh, or a horse standing that shifts from one foot to another.

In that leisure, Time became non-existent. To me, at any rate, it seems less real than space, though both are vague enough. The past is never quite past. If the Athenians, so long ago, had acted differently, some ramification, some untraceable divergence would have affected the lives of all of us —even mine, as I swam in the sun. There is a bond of past and future, with us between them, and every act, moving from one into the other, changes the world as it does so. The atomic age has in fact been with us always, since the first deed started the first consequence on its way.

The religions of our day believe that all things move in eternity creating a responsibility which, if it were felt with conviction, might influence the conduct of men. It might make us either immobile like the sea-urchin, or good. The Greeks, in an unsafe and a mysterious world, held to a lesser road—to the things their ancestors had taught them, the reputation and the approval of their friends. This rendered the same person startlingly unexpected, heroic or kind or cruel, according to what faced him at the moment. And even

Chios

Socrates, when he gave his vote for the six generals could not be comforted as we are by the sight of his act going down the centuries for ever, adding a small positive momentum to the direction of everything that exists.

SAMOS

The Double Code

There is no law that can stand between a man and his enemy.

EURIPIDES, Ion.

Why this leaping at random between hate and love?

EURIPIDES, Women of Troy.

WHEN HE REALISED THAT THE ATHENIAN CAUSE WAS lost, Conon with the eight ships that were under him sailed away while he could, for the open sea and the south, where a Greek in Cyprus was his friend. But before he went, while the enemy was still busy on the conquered shore of Aegospotami, he put in across the straits to Abarnis. Here the Spartans kept their tall cruising sails; and, loading them up to hinder the pursuit, he made away.

But Lysander, when he had gathered the triremes and executed the Athenian sailors, and brought in the northern cities round the straits, sailed slowly south to Mitylene, and on to Athens, already beleaguered by land. And many shiploads of unhappy people preceded him, for he had given safe conduct to Athens to all who wished to go, knowing that it would starve the sooner: and all who belonged to Athens, the colonists (cleruchs) who had been settled on the unwilling islands, and the merchants and ships from their harbours, all left the shores now hostile and made for the crowded city. And all the Greek world had fallen away from the Athenians immediately after the battle, with the exception of Samos; there the people had slaughtered the aristocrats and held possession of their city; and the Athenians in gratitude bestowed their citizenship—no longer so happy a possession—on all the Samians.

The Samians had been too deeply implicated in democracy to cherish any hopes from Lysander. They had provided the headquarters for the Athenian forces during all the eight years that had passed since the tragedy of Syracuse—ever since Strombichides, the Athenian admiral, arrived in 412 B.C. with eight ships and, quickly conscripting one Samian vessel, sailed to Teos and required them to remain quiet. At that time, seven years before Aegospotami, the Samians rose against the upper classes, took their lands and houses, put to death some two hundred and banished four hundred, and forbade intermarriage with their daughters; while Alcibiades—nominally on the Spartan side—began to advise Tissaphernes 'not to be in too great a hurry to end the war or to . . . put the power by land and sea into the same hands'; and, getting into touch with the Athenians in Samos, or they with him, declared that if there were an oligarchy in Athens in the place of the rascally democracy that had banished him, he would be glad to return to his country and make Tissaphernes their friend.

The oligarchy was established in Athens, but Alcibiades was unable to provide the friendship and alliance with Persia which was its aim; and in Samos, when it came to the point, neither the Athenian army nor the local population could

stomach the loss of the only form of administration in which
they had ever had a part. The Athenian soldiers and the
Samians banded together, against Persia, Sparta and their own
government in Athens too—whose envoys, learning how
matters stood, 'remained in Delos'. It was under these circumstances that Alcibiades became general of the Athenians
in Samos.

We too were now making for Samos in *Elfin*, not across
open water like Conon, but eastward under the mainland
where the ugly slopes of Corycus, once infamous for pirates,
run empty to the sea. Here there are no valleys, but merely
scoopings of shallow floods in the limestone; the shelter of
Injir lies deep and safe and the little Macres peninsula beyond
it. Then comes the wide opening of the bay of Teos, so
lonely that, after the first world war, the Greeks were able
to land here unopposed; and Myonnesus, where, long before
the Roman-Rhodian battle made it famous, a Spartan admiral
landed to butcher his prisoners in 427 B.C. The Samian exiles
told him that 'he was not going the right way to free Hellas
in massacring men who had never raised a hand against him,
and would turn many more friends into enemies than enemies
into friends'.[1]

In the shelter of the headland that had hidden the Rhodian
ships we spent a night, in a small inlet where warm springs
ooze through beds of yellow flowers; and, in the morning,
continued our coasting voyage, by Lebedus whose cultivated
slopes lie in the lap of the wooded Gallesus, where the slit
through to Smyrna can now be negotiated in one and a half
hours with tanks. The first operation of NATO was staged
here for combined manœuvres. The stones of a low fortified
promontory are still visible, with waves almost washing their
foundations, absurdly vulnerable at all times. It was a for-
bidden area till 1953, and almost deserted, except for a hamlet
in fields that continue strung thinly between the mountains

and the sea, until the high eastern cliff of Notium appears. There Alcibiades' battle took place, in 406 B.C. The main Athenian fleet, a hundred ships, was drawn up round the estuary of the 'coldest river in Ionia', out of sight of Lysander and his ninety Spartan triremes hauled up to be dried and repaired on the shore of Ephesus close by.

Our route continued to criss-cross with these ancient dramas, and the *Elfin* spent some uncomfortable hours at Kushadasi, the port of Ephesus—unable to land since our papers bound us for Samos, but delayed by the necessity of dropping Mehmet the cook, who had to give evidence at a trial.

It was due next day, and Mehmet was called as a witness, but, being one of our crew, had no document to enable him to land this side of Samos. In this perplexity, I suggested to D. B. that a letter to the Commandant of Police might allow them to do what they liked with the problem. This had the happiest results. Mehmet departed with officially blessed irregularity, and I was encouraged in the belief that it is only when I am absent that D. B. gets into trouble on a coast. Meanwhile we tossed in a miserable way in the lee of a small island with a castle which is all the shelter that Kushadasi can offer; and, late in the afternoon, sailed under livid, tumultuous clouds by the steep of Mycale to Samos.

Many ages are memorable in Samos, where Epicurus was said to have been educated and Homer entertained as a guest, and Socrates learned philosophy from Archelaus, and Aristarchus—the Copernicus of the ancient world—was born.[2] Sophocles served here in a siege in which Pericles commanded.[3] This was in 440 B.C., when the Samian gentry already looked to Persia for help; and Artemon, an engineer of Clazomenae, made engines 'such as those called rams and tortoises' for the Greeks. The invention (old in Assyria but new to the west) spread rapidly from Samos: city walls, built in that age without mortar, fell down. Within thirty-one years, the earlier

Vathy

Hannibal at Selinunte was using battering-rams and towers far exceeding the city walls in height.[4]

But the mind, in Samos, returns most willingly to that short time before the downfall of Athens, when the island was the centre of history for a while. For events are images of the characters that made them; and the Samian character has not greatly changed: its present and its past fit together. As we sailed by in *Elfin* in the dusk, a white blur showed the monastery from which, when Leros in the last war had fallen, and the islands were in danger, the Archbishop rode down at night on mule-back to a caique waiting in the shadow below. Eighty-two Athenian ships had once lain here and made, as we were making, for Tigani.[5] There was no splash of oars now in the channel as *Elfin* slid along it. The long snouts of Mycale stretched westward, uninhabited but gentle, and the outline of Miletus showed parallel in the south.

The night fell. We glided under the Samian hills, dark green with spring. The surface of the water was caught by moonlight, as if a crowd of golden sickles were harvesting its darkness. And we slept by the quay of Tigani, among the caiques, with their nets hung from the masts to dry.

The island, next morning, showed itself full of villages and vineyards. We drove to Vathy, the capital, a town of ten thousand people, neat and sharply tilted round a sea-promenade that lines a northern bay. Here, even during the German occupation, the citizens walked up and down in the evenings, waiting for their fortunes to change. D. B. knew the town well, having served there during the brief British occupation o the island in 1943, and knew the Archbishop who lived there in his palace—an old man, learned and talkative, with a white beard, and white hair so faded that it was streaked with yellow, tied with black ribbon at his back. He sat in a high room, with straight red velvet chairs against its walls; and in touch with him, in the town, lived Mr. Louis Marc, the honorary

British Consul, with his brother. He had been consul for many years, and his father, grandfather, and great-grandfather before him—since 1818; wherefore the Germans destroyed seven of their houses out of spite. Now the younger generation cannot find consular employment and the dynasty with its tradition will end; and with it the advantage of representatives disinterested and respected and *not to be moved* from the island; and if I had any influence, and if influence would help —which we are too Sabbatarian to allow—how gladly would I use it, if only to prove that the sabbath was made for men and not men for the regulations, and that devoted service is something for which human laws can profitably suffer a certain amount of strain.

This is all in the tradition of the island that ransomed the Athenian prisoners in the days of Xerxes: and, before that, in the 6th century, saved the children in a temple of Artemis when the Corinthian Periander was sending them from Corfu as eunuchs to the Lydian court. 'And when the Corinthians would have prevented the boys from getting food, the Samians appointed a festival which they still keep after the same fashion ... dances of damsels and young men after nightfall; and made it a custom that they should bring cates of sesame seed and honey, so that the Corcyreian boys might seize them and have food; and this went on till the keepers of the boys left them and departed.'

In the wars of the Greek liberation, in 1821, a rough and hasty fortress was built near the older Venetian castle; a few marble columns stand about it and the whitewashed church is beside it, to which people were winding in procession, praying to be spared earthquakes, with their icons under their arms. There is always a choice of things to pray about, in the islands.

A more lavish atmosphere of prayer, ostentatious and decayed, hangs about the temple of Hera, which was one of the three wonders that made Herodotus prolong his words about the Samians. His mole of twenty fathoms has disappeared. His conduit for water, built in the 6th century by an engineer of Megara, was rediscovered in 1878. A finely built passage, narrower than Herodotus describes it, with pointed ceiling of smooth sloping stones, digs its ancient way into the hill, and a little marble temple among cistus and rosemary greets its emergence, with an inscription set up by Themistocles Sophoulis of Samos, who led the 1912 revolution and became prime minister of Greece.

The temple, the third wonder, never finished, lies deserted as it was seen by Cicero and Strabo, far on the western crescent of the bay. It looks across, with one white column standing, to the blue Fujiyama shape of Mycale, across the strait; and the slabs of the Sacred Way that led to it are lost in pools of swampy rushes. A Byzantine church and a few small buildings, which Strabo saw filled with works of ancient art,[6] lie heaped about with that edited look which archaeology gives to ruins, for the Germans were digging here for long before the war. But the temple eludes them. Immense, with nothing left but the stylobate and the bases of its columns, and the traces of two great altars before the eastern steps—with wild gladioli and rushes seeping in bog about it—it holds the landscape—the half-bowl of the mountains, the fields of corn and flowers, the pale blue of Mycale and far Miletus, the dark blue of the sea, and the smooth curve of shore beside the Sacred Way; and it holds them not with the picture of what was there before, but with a simple magnificence of ruin. The vitality of the old tyrant, Polycrates, is still in it, in the dimensions which he imagined and in the ruthlessness with which vast drums of columns and bases, the work of older craftsmen, were pushed underground to build his new foundations out of sight. The first temple was built by Rhoecus and Theodore of Samos, and was burnt in 530 B.C. and the new one was interrupted in a drastic way by the crucifixion of Polycrates himself. Then the Persian wars, and the revolt from Athens, and trouble continuously: the columns of the outer colonnade were never finished, and those of the southern side, put up after Alexander, were never fluted nor roofed. The series of steps on the sides were never built, so that the temple, high in the swamp, must have looked as if it stood on a podium; and though the 2nd century A.D. swept up to the eastern end with a flight of ten steps, these were merely a background for two mediocre little shrines close to the ancient altar, between the entrance and the Sacred Way.[7]

The temple stands, shorn of all that was intended to complete it, like a dream; but it lives, too, like a dream. Half sunk in water, a few of the column bases lie aslant, six feet or more across, with deep and solid carving; and the great altar, which the archaeologists with laborious piety had almost reconstructed, lies tumbled in a second ruin, pulled down by the young men of Samos, who disliked the Germans at the end of the war.

It is a pity, and strangely endearing too: for the young men were free of doubts, and to become so is the aim of all our journey. But it is better not to overlook the preliminaries, when doubts are, if not virtue, perhaps transition towards virtue—paralysing unless they lead towards certainty, but indispensable till certainty is in sight. We need their tentative assurance, though we long for a time when we can be secure without them. The young men of Samos, if they thought at all, assumed that this time had come; it happens to people who believe what they are told; and it is what also deflected the ancient Greek world when the mainland governments took it over, and the Ionian humility was lost, and curiosity grew dangerous.

A double morality

This was after the flush of the 5th century, when the governments felt that they knew what the gods were after. They found certitudes where the Ionian philosophers, and Socrates later, could look only for distant, possibly unattainable, hopes. And with their gods the governments of the late 5th century also took for granted the most fatal of all things—a code of ethics rigid from the past. In its double morality the seeds of decay lay hidden.

The code taught that it was disgraceful to be outdone by enemies in cruelty or by friends in kindness; and this was universally accepted. It was Xenophon's idea of the obvious, and Isocrates' too. It was a commonplace, an axiom of the time. Socrates assumed it, and Plato's doubts came slowly. 'The majority of men always believe that the right advice ... is ... such action as will do the greatest possible harm to one's enemies and the greatest possible good to one's friends; whereas it is by no means easy to do much harm to others without also suffering ... oneself.'[8]

The compassion of the Lord's Prayer has replaced the double Greek code. Yet they did what they could with what they had; and, unlike us, believed and acted upon it; and could be cruel with a clear conscience while they trusted their code.

Socrates offended by being above its range—with personal benefit or injury out of sight; and Alcibiades, standing below the level of his day, was criticized for the opposite reason.[9] If I were to select two episodes to justify his unpopularity in his lifetime, I would first take the account of his sailing with all his ships to Cyme, to hurl false charges against the Cymaeans, when he wished to have an excuse for plundering their territory: 'and the Cymaeans despatched an embassy to Athens and denounced Alcibiades for having laid waste an allied city which had done no wrong.'

And secondly I would take the story of how 'Diomedes, one

of his friends, had sent in his care a four-horse team to Olympia;
and Alcibiades, when entering it in the usual way, listed the
horses as his own; and when he was the victor in the
four-horse race . . . took for himself the glory of the victory
and did not return the horses to the man who had entrusted
them to his care.'

These acts were below the contemporary level. Injuries to
enemies, the betrayal of his city, the Greek could pardon:
'the true lover of his country is not he who consents to lose
it unjustly rather than attack it, but he who longs for it so much
that he will go all lengths to recover it':[10] most of the 5th
century exiles could agree with that. What was difficult to
overlook, was that the gentle side of the code was omitted;
Alcibiades' kindness was restricted to himself.

Even when properly observed, this code could not hold its
world for long. The constant reason for Greek failure lay in
the double morality which separated enemies from friends.
Alexander, because he overleapt it, was able to establish the
Hellenistic world about us, through his solitary thought; and
many churches since, with charities however incomplete, have
stood where governments fell. Through near two thousand
years, the code has in theory been superseded and our cruelties
are now no longer committed with such clear cheerfulness as in
the greatness of Greece. The average man might still vote for
the death of an enemy; but the commandment on which
Christianity is based would impinge on his mind, and such
deeds are now done at a cost to integrity which is in itself
sufficient to banish tranquillity from the soul. For it is certain
that there can be no happiness if the things we believe in are
different from the things we do.

But the young men of Samos, and Philocles the general,
who thought nothing of cutting off the hands of captives and
threw the crews of vessels over rocks, and went so gaily to his

end, are not unhappy: their acts and their beliefs are one. They stand confident on the raft of their morality, not noticing that its immobility is illusion, nor knowing that there is no choice between staying or going but only a choice of direction, and that to halt in the stability of one's fathers is to let the rudder drift out of one's hand. To think to keep things as they are, is to let them move unpredictably, since nothing but death will still the beat of the heart or keep the universe from its perpetual motion: and this strange effort of humanity to break the progress of Time with pauses has caused practically every revolution in history and the fall of many empires beside the Athenian. Yet the choice of direction remains, nor was it long before the grimness of events and the logic of their own minds brought the Greeks to seek it, beyond the static pattern of their rules.

Travellers and sailors are nearer than governments to the meaning of events. They have no such illusions of stability. They know that nothing made of paper or of any other substance will keep the world quiet. They see their pilgrimage under the arc of a wider necessity, lit by horizons that change and never end. From the high edge of Samos, where no roads are yet cut, we looked into the light of the afternoon, over the warm sea. Many islands lay there, stretching to west and south—Icaria, the Phournoi, Lipsos and Patmos, Leros, and Calymnos far away; and the Great Man-eater, Megalos Anthropophagos, a solitary rock waist-high in the sea. The light seemed to melt, as if it were eating the islands; it lay heavy like the sheaves of a yellow harvest made of air, flattened into wide smooth circles by the sun. A timeless, motionless eternity seemed to hold it; the gossip of the waves, the small white edges breaking, went on unseen below. The same illusion of quietness, the same perpetual motion. High up here, four thousand feet high, the Samian sentries must have seen Conon with his eight ships, and the captured sails on board that kept them safe—small as beetles, working their banks of oars, and making for the south.

4

PATMOS TO CALYMNOS

Time

No mortal ought
To challenge Time.　　　EURIPIDES, Bacchae.

FROM CHESHME, ONE MORNING AT THE END OF SEPTEMBER we too made south, for Patmos. It was the *Elfin's* adventure—her first thirteen hours at a stretch of open sailing. We set out in a subsiding swell, through wide waves blotched with dark undulations like pythons coiling and uncoiling in the sun. Presently they sank; the sea, under the height of the morning, fluttered with ripples.

Elfin's engines purred gently; her flanks eased themselves into unnoticeable valleys with tiny creaking noises: free of the hillsides that had bred her timbers, she delighted to move in the lap of the water and quiver as it touched her, as her leaves had once quivered to the winds. She flapped her yellow sail to the headland airs as we passed the tip of Chios. The eastern promontories receded; the faint wraith of Samos showed ahead. It grew to the buffalo shape of the island, that plunges to 150 fathoms within a quarter of a mile of the shore, and slopes on into the hollow, near 700 fathoms, of the Icarian Sea.

There in the hot afternoon *Elfin* stopped and floated, while we swam in water whose darkness lay solid, like a sapphire tombstone unexpectedly transparent, between one's toes and chin.

Now we sailed under the rock-built height of the island, flashing with unseen windows of villages high up in the sun; past Icaria, pale silver, on which Greek communists live in

31

exile—most primitive of islands, where a hundred years ago
a four-post bed was burnt in the market place as a dangerous
innovation,[1] and Randolph describes the winter grapes round
and red between the rocks, and fishermen rowing naked to
save their clothes. We skirted Phournoi, near on the right,
with barren fjords. Faint, almost invisible in the east, were
Mycale's double peaks and the wide emptiness of Maeander;
south-west the Great Man-eater rock, and the toothed outline
of Patmos ahead.

Sailing up here from Cilicia and then westward, with horses
and foot-soldiers and six hundred galleys, 'past Icarus across the
Aegean', the Persian armament moved to Marathon. Here,
earliest among all the islands, Samos bought four ships from
Corinth—the first place in Hellas where triremes were built
in the 8th century seafaring;[2] here they sailed forth in long
ships and seized the bronze bowl that was meant for the Lydian
king and dedicated it in the temple of Hera, and began a war
with Sparta. We were in the Samian sea.

The evening shone green and yellow around us. Far and
near islands appeared flattened like book-pressed roses; only
the long Icarian ridge still lay as if about to break to a golden
dust on the path of the sun.

Presently, in a world that had grown transparent and fine
as aquamarine to await her, the moon stepped over a cliff,
on to the dancing floor of the sea. We were near Patmos.
A bay was opening before us, so wide that its far end was out
of sight. Low cliffs stood round it like fields of moonlit
flowers. Through the pale water, *Elfin* moved almost silent,
her engines shod with velvet. A sort of ecstasy held us, born
of those harmonies and our safety amongst them—the open
sea and the day's voyage behind us, and night folding itself
upon us, with another day beyond. I sat on the little deck,
in the kind night air, and thought of the human journey also—
what madness that thinks to arrest it, and longs for unattain-

32

able stillness, and strives to break with unnatural permanence this ancient procession of time? How dreary for the gods to watch us, like Ferdinand in the bull-ring—put here in the arena, and anxious only to sit! And what cowardice is ours to think the universe so meagre that we dare not trust its unknown to be better than the known: for what has ever yet approached so near perfection as to be unattainable to men?

Now, the Athenian Empire has fallen, and the peak of the classic age is past, and we are making for a modern world—an age as they call it of transition, as if every age that ever has been were not transition, till Time must end? And Time we can neither stop nor start, but only steer: direction only is given us to hold.

The source of political trouble lies in this confusion between the mastery and the direction of time. The very words of progress and reaction presuppose a control which is not there. The timid, who wish to keep what they are moving away from and fear all motion, and the rash, who wish to think that motion is enough without direction—are alike forgetful that they stand not on the river bank but in the stream. On a raft too, not on an island. All is open to them, except stability. Beyond their static illusion, they have the earth to move about in: to find a way for it is all their business, and Time, through which they guide it, is their sea.

What fate can be more godlike? In this liberty, the past is our treasure. Its works, whether we know them or not, flourish in our lives with whatever strength they had. From it we draw provision for our journey, the collected wisdom whose harvests are all ours to reap and carry with us, though we may never live again in the fields that grew them.

As if in answer to these reflections, the *Elfin* turned a corner and the high monastery on its hill shone, lit with electricity in the moonlight. The lower monastery of St. John shone too, half way on the slope below. They sparkled like heavenly

33

battlements above the dimness through which we floated—
our night that was neither light nor shadow, where the coast
lay empty under the moon. A long black jagged ridge of rock
ran ahead of us, and as we passed beyond it, the illuminated
height became human—a parent monastery with a quiet, white
country harbour asleep at its feet.

As we climbed next morning up the polished worn stones
of the old causeway between the loops of the new road, D. B.
prepared me for a possibly cool reception by the monks above.
In the days of his activity as an orthodox ecclesiastic in Athens,
or possibly earlier on Mount Athos, D. B. had known the
Spiritual Director of Patmos.

I find, in my diary, a rather summary description of D. B.
and his family as I first met them in Smyrna. 'He has,' I
wrote, 'run through several religions and is now secularized,
having come to the conclusion that the world is just one of
God's mistakes. There is an enchanting little daughter and
his wife is unsubmissive, devoted, hates untidiness and anti-
quity, and has a charming smile. He tells me the war released
him from his monastic life just in time.'

This is not an adequate description either of his family or
of D. B., the pleasantness and kindness of whose character will
appear more and more as our voyage continues; but it explains
why we walked up with uncertainty ahead, pausing on our
way to visit St. John the Divine in his cave, where the revela-
tion split the rock in three places and the cracks still show.

The stone, worn by the Saint's hand in prayer and his head
in sleep, makes the ceiling of a church endowed by Anna
Comnena when centuries had passed. Now a seminary
flourishes, and new dormitories were building for three hundred students who come from all over Greece and the islands.
They remain from the age of twelve for ten years, and then
many go on to Athens University, to the theological school.

They received us, as they do in the islands, with the manners

34

of hosts at home. When we left them, we continued to climb to the village, and at the top of it entered the monastery, by a flagged slope and zigzag way under arches, beside small chapels and through fortress walls. Tall battlements of many periods hold a warren of rooms and stone-paved corridors, arched doors and vaulted ceilings, all whitewashed, with pools and profiles of shadows. In the centre is a refectory and a vast marble table scooped with niches, one for each inmate in more prosperous times to keep his glass and napkin: the middle of the table is lower, so that it can be washed down easily, and an earthenware bowl to hold about thirty gallons stands four-handled in a corner for food.

When in A.D. 1045 the monks had to leave Heraclea under Latmus, the abbot Christodulos came to Patmos and founded his monastery, and he is buried in the church whose dusky interior, rich with icons, embroidery and jewels, opens by a frescoed portico, to a little cobbled court like a well in the shadow of the buildings—where a monk was drawing water from the real well among all his pots of aromatic herbs. He led us by many passages and devious stairs to the library, and there the Spiritual Director, who is also the librarian, came to greet D. B., thinking him a stranger.

He walked very slim and light towards us, his grey eyes clever and kind, his beard neither black nor white against the long black gown, but bright like speckled granite under a waterfall. As he looked at D. B., who began to explain who he was, the fine old face showed one emotion after another—surprise, spontaneous pleasure, a wave of careful observation, and at last a look of pure human love and understanding—with which he kissed him, and they talked in great peace of this and that.

He showed us the manuscripts; the deeds granted by Alexis Comnenus; the lamp that had belonged to the conqueror of Constantinople—a strange relic in this place. But the greatest treasure of Patmos is a 5th-century gospel written on purple

35

parchment in clear round letters of silver, with the divine names all in gold.

Two or three monks joined us as we drank coffee with the abbot. Their ages varied, their beards went through every shade from dark to white, but their eyes all had the same soft brown Byzantine look, as if the monastery were nothing but the inside of one of its own missals come to life.

From its roof, crowded with white turrets and hexagonal tiled domes, the whole of Patmos lay in sight: the village below us pressed against our battlements, with machicolated streets, carved stone doors and windows, and a paved piazza under tamarisk trees where the slope turned down.

The vineyards were beyond, rounded like breasts on the curves of the hills, and wasp-waisted promontories lay between the western and eastern bays. 'In the Candy warr, the Venetian Armado, almost the whole fleet, lay here to winter ... but since that time, the Turk on the one hand and the Privateers on the other, have brought them so low that now they are as miserable as any.' All lay quiet and uneventful in the sun, resting from its histories.

In the afternoon we left Patmos and sailed away by Leros, where Randolph saw about twenty very great marble pillars entire, too far from the sea to be carried away. Its very rocks now look blasted by the war. When the Italians, after the 1943 armistice, let Rhodes fall into the German hand, the British in Leros were doomed, for there was no aircraft to keep the enemy out of that sky. The Germans were very few in Rhodes, though they had the armour: their general was on the point of surrendering when his A.D.C. begged him to wait: the Italian surrender was already on its way. The result was the shambles of Leros.

Almost touching it in the south, Calymnos, colonized by Dorians of Epidauros, now held the evening. Its gentler valleys were out of sight except for two hamlets: their stray lights began to shine among trees, but the cliffs soon shut them away; and the *Elfin*, small and persevering, chugged for hours under uninhabited heights, whose precipices fall steep into the moonlit water. Their tall chasms, curtained with shadow upon shadow, shone in high places with a dusky brilliance, like negroes' shoulders jutting beneath the moon and the only whiteness was the edge of the foam that bit them. The sea was immensely lonely between the islands, the world deserted. In three days from Chios we had met one caique only, making north from Rhodes to Smyrna, bringing charcoal: our Cretan skipper's son was on it, and shouted the news of the south.

The traffic of the past too grew rare, except for unrecorded flittings of pirates. They forced the towns to move inland and produced the lonely shores. Even in the wildest centuries, the Aegean here must have held its spell of beauty, its solitary peace. Pursuing or pursued, the little boats hugged cliffs to hide in creeks or shadows—and the loveliness and idleness held them while they waited for the passing of their danger, of weather or of men.

One can understand why they now love the electric light in their harbours: its welcome looks warm and safe to seafaring people used to the barren slopes. It takes the place of waters and gardens, and lights up for the approaching sailor the thickets of masts and nets thrown over painted prows that mean his people's harvest, and behind them the crowded houses of the hillside of his friends. Not green things growing nor the sound of water falling, but light—the brightest possible —is the island ornament.

So Calymnos appeared, with its Italian palace in the harbour; and houses with flat roofs packed together, washed pale Hellenic blue to annoy Germans and Italians; and high sidewalks with outlets for floods under the quayside esplanade. All was glitteringly lit and well-cared-for but deserted, for the quays are empty and the households presumably in bed by 9 p.m.

Patmos to Calymnos

For months of the spring and summer the sailors of Calymnos are away fishing for sponges. Most of their boats now have a diver's outfit to fish in deep waters, but I have watched men off the coast of Benghazi still sinking down naked with a knife in their hand and a stone at their wrist. They can stay two minutes under water, and their friends haul them up quickly at the tug of the cord.

One wonders how the aqualung will affect this ancient trade. In Calymnos it was declining. During the war, the population dropped from thirty-nine to three thousand, and had now recovered to about half its former figure. The permit to fish off Cyrenaica had been withdrawn for the first time for centuries, and the Bahamas' sponges were diseased. In a neat house on the quay, the chief merchants told us this story, sitting under a portrait of Mr. Gladstone (for they are British subjects though Greeks of the island). The consul in Rhodes, they added, had left them to a German concentration camp while he departed. Ashamed and sorrowful, we sat under a Victorian picture of a full House of Commons, and felt that something was wrong with our status in the Aegean.

The atmosphere of fate is noticeable in islands: the abruptness of space, so sharply cut off, is a constant reminder. It clothes the everyday life in symbols. In Calymnos, the sponge-fishers told me, their wives accompany them to the quayside when they set out in the spring: and when all the men have departed, the women gather round their fountain, and put a black kerchief on their heads instead of a white one, to wear till their men come home.

Euripides makes Cassandra speak of the happiness of Ilium, where those who survived in battle returned every evening to their wives and children, and whose dead—prepared for burial by the hands they loved—were laid to rest in the ground that gave them birth. This ritual continuity belongs to the Mediterranean where the Mother Goddess was worshipped, and it

38

seems to me strange that chivalrous feeling should so often be assumed to be characteristic only of the north.

The Greek goddesses, particularly Hera, had much in common with the Victorian idea of women—an idea shared by every age that concentrates on the differences and not on the likenesses of the sexes. It produces chivalry; and it seems to me not altogether a feminine advantage that it has been superseded, and that the similarities are now so much more emphasized than the differences that some women and far too many men seem to be unaware of any divergence at all. The woman's difference turns her too into a symbol, a refuge where life is potentially nourished or sheltered, a window out of time, however humble, towards the secret of duration and life. To be so considered makes up for a number of inconveniences.

As for men, the neglect of chivalry is the loss of their oldest and strongest service, and it is not particularly helpful to them. It often provided them with the only unselfishness they had. The obvious altruism of a home can still save the women; but committees or even philanthropy are usually poor idols in cold shrines for the men: and the Mother Goddess makes the wives of Calymnos and their husbands as much happier than we are, as the Trojans were happier than their enemies 'buried in alien earth'.

One such lies in Calymnos beneath the dusty fig and wind-swept almond trees, by a ruined monastery on the side of the valley, where the old walled town was built at the top of a triple precipice out of the way of pirates. It is little more than a century since the people abandoned it, but the ruins—heaped with shapeless walls—might belong to any time. A piece of marble column might come from anywhere. Only a shield, with a coat of arms built above a cistern, shows that there was some sort of habitation in the crusading age.

Seven or eight whitewashed chapels with barrel roofs are still kept in repair. To them, during the war, an English fugitive crept from some shipwreck. The villagers fed him and hid him there without understanding his language, until one day they found him dead and buried him. The Greek Anthology is full of such sailors, and every gulf and headland must have known them. But I have read the epitaphs, since I came home, with a deeper meaning, dedicating them anew as it were to this fellow countryman and to those who miss him, in his unknown grave.

'O smiling mariners . . . tell his father Meno that he lies by the Icarian rocks, having given up the ghost in the Aegean sea.'

5

ISLAND PIRATES

Adventure

The lone sailor Nauplius
Lit his false fire on the Capherian cape.   EURIPIDES, Helen.

EVER SINCE OUR BATHE IN THE DEEP WATER, HÜSEYIN THE skipper had been carrying something in his mind. He came round to it in an oriental manner by telling D. B. the story of four men and their horse, who were overturned in a boat between Calymnos and Cos and eaten by a shark. The shark then felt ill, and leaned against the island to die; and one of the hooves from the shipwreck, a watch, a piece of flannel and other easily recognized oddments were discovered inside him.

We thought this a mere moral tale intended to discourage us from swimming in the open sea; but as we were slipping south again next afternoon, with Calymnos elongated on the horizon, D. B. called me up quickly from my siesta on the narrow seat which was my bed at night and my bench at table in the daytime. I was clever by now at the in-and-out movement which landed one, across an overhang, on *Elfin's* deck,

41

and D. B. was still able to point to a splutter of foam in the distance—a nine-foot shark he told me—that had swum under our bows and was now enjoying himself about half a mile away. It was his tail that was lashing up the foam, making a fountain of it as if he were a French taxi-driver in Paradise—alone and big in the Place de la Concorde and everything around him small. One could imagine the frightened pedestrian fish underwater giving a wide liberty to his robust delight; while, above the surface, the arching drops fell in cascades that looked as if they tinkled, into a smooth silence of sun and sea and islands, a meridian solitude of light.

Hüseyin in the placid afternoon hours sat at the wheel with his head aslant and his thin old bones bunched comfortably in clothes from which his talent for shabbiness had long ago rubbed away any consular lustre. It was a pain to D. B. to see what Hüseyin could do to a new suit in a matter of hours; and then to watch him amble away in harbour, one gym shoe untied and the other half off, one sleeve up and the other down, his open neck disclosing strange underwear, and what he had on turning out not to be his port suit at all, but the old dungarees of last year. Into their frayed pockets he would try to press the *Elfin*'s papers and our passports, on his way to visit the harbour-master and police with the Prestige of Britain behind him. What this meant, D. B. would explain in that voluminous Greek language that pours and coils and flashes. And where, anyway, *was* the suit purposely given for these occasions?

Hüseyin, whom nothing could perturb except the weather, would smile his one-toothed smile, dive into the recess of *Elfin* that it was more restful not to investigate, and reappear in a Best already crumpled and doomed but at least intact. He would then shuffle off with the air of a nanny who has kept her child quiet for half an hour and, burrowing in and out of the quayside offices, shuffle out again with all the

42

necessary formalities accomplished. For he knew everyone, and every port; and the creeks and rocks between the ports, and every cranny of the Aegean. He was a Muhammedan Turk of Crete—whatever that may mean—and of the tribe of Odysseus' sailors. He would have sat comfortably on their benches and found himself at home, for he too knew the vicissitudes of fortune. He had risen to the ownership of a caique, and it had caught fire, and sunk, uninsured, while he watched it, in the bay of Trigyllion, on Mycale, where St. Paul touched on his way to Miletus. Then he had gone into partnership, and watched another boat sink slowly through neglect in Fethiye harbour, and so had been obliged to go back to other owners; and gave his money to a fat wife who lived on land and spent it and asked for more. These things too were like the weather: they came and went on the surface and required their moments of attention, but that was as far as they had penetrated. Often, as I looked at the bald head—brown and polished as if it were waxed—and at the face wrinkled by the sea just as the rocks were wrinkled, and the sailor's eyes that had a smile in them pale and impersonal as that of the sea—the reflection rather of some smile far out of sight—I would wonder what it was that did penetrate? Whatever it was, it belonged to the Aegean; taken away from its incidents, its moods, gossip and variety, Hüseyin would die just as the beduin of the desert dies in prison: there is perhaps a freedom that flourishes below the conscious level; and the people who have it live by it although they do not know that it is there.

The Cretans were almost as famous for piracy as the Cilicians in their time, and I used sometimes to wonder what circumstances could turn a man as sweet-natured as Hüseyin into a pirate. It could be done, no doubt, if the injustice of the world were sufficiently strong. The Mediterranean seems never to have been entirely free from piracy except in our own age and in the early centuries of the Roman Empire; as late as 1905 the German sailing handbook remarks that it is unsafe to keep too close to north Africa—and yet the Hüseyins of all the ages must have been fundamentally the same as they are now. There were better and worse times, the safety by sea corresponding to the prosperity on land. Crete, with the Minoan navy to protect her, could leave its island unguarded except on the north; under the Athenian Empire, the walls of seaboard cities were left unbuilt or sometimes—as at Chios—demolished. In the 5th century 'Ionia was unfortified', and Thucydides and Diodorus mention specifically Rhodes, Cos, Cnidus and Clazomenae, Samos, Mitylene, Lampsacus and Cyzicus among the unprotected towns. With the Spartan supremacy, which was unadapted to the sea, the pirates returned. They served, indeed, in the victorious fleet, and one of them, Theopompus of Miletus, carried the news of Aegospotami to Sparta.[1]

Isocrates complains of pirates in the 4th century, and remarks that it was unsafe to send to the Hellespont while Sparta commanded at sea. One could get 30 per cent on a loan for the voyage there and back from Athens, so great was the risk of loss.[2] When Athens recovered, there was an improvement, and an Athenian squadron was cruising about on police duty on the eve of Alexander's departure for Asia. In 315-14 B.C., Thymochares, one of her captains, reduced the pirate Glaucetas of Cythnos, and this was the last act of Athens as guardian. Alexander took over the task. His admiral in 331 was told to clear the seas;[3] but during the wars that followed the conqueror's death, the distinction between pirate and mercenary became more wavering than ever. In 302 B.C. we are told that eight thousand 'light armed troops and freebooters' joined the army of Demetrius; and the general of Lysmachius used a pirate's ship to capture Ephesus, loading it with pretended handcuffed captives who were really Macedonian soldiers.

The Cretans

When Alexander's admiral began his operations, he started with Crete, whose inhabitants had a poor reputation from Homer onwards and were considered by Herodotus as particularly expert in kidnapping the women of Asia. Their actual hunting grounds lay in the seas where we and *Elfin* were sailing, and here they continued through the centuries, along the route of the north and south Aegean traffic.

'They go,' says Mr. Roberts in 1692, who was captured by them, 'for the Furnes [Phournoi] and lie there under the high Land hid, having a watch on the Hill with a little Flag, whereby they make a Signal, if they see any Sail: they slip out and lie athwart the Boak of Samos, and take their Prize; they lie in the same nature under Necaria [Icaria] . . . in the Spring and forepart of the Summer. Then for the middle of the Summer, they ply on the coast of Cyprus; and if they hear the least noise of any Algerines and Grand Turks ships at Rhodes, away they scour for the coast of Alexandria and Damiata, being shole Water, well knowing the Turks will not follow them thither. The latter part of the Summer they come stealing on the Coast of Syria, where they do most mischief with their Feleucca, which commonly rows with 12 Ores and carries 6 Sitters: For at Night they leave the Ship, and get under the Shoar before Day, and go ashoar, where they waylay the Turks . . . From hence towards the Autumn they come lurking about the Islands . . . until they put in also to lie up in the winter.'

It was only the Cilicians who were able to hold the sea all the year round, and later on the British, who 'keep the sea even in midwinter . . . thanks to the handiness of their ships and the skill of their mariners'.

But the earlier pirates with their smaller boats would catch coasting vessels on their way up from southern Asia Minor, or sheltering from the north wind in the lee of Icaria or Samos on their way from the Cyclades eastward, where from Siphnos for instance, the town on a high hill, Randolph says that the inhabitants see several islands at a great distance and often are diverted with sea-fights; and at Melos the privateers continually bring some presents to the Capuchins who have a convent there.[4]

Samos, which lay on the direct route of traffic, became so raided for supplies by the pirates that the whole population allowed the Genoese to remove them and resettle them in Chios; though they themselves were said to have spent ten years on Mycale living by piracy when driven from their island in more ancient days, a fact which they commemorated by a festival dedicated to Hermes, in which theft was legalized.

It was no simple matter for men in boats to recognize their danger, for any travelling sailors might become pirates on occasion if the circumstances were favourable—like those three Athenian ambassadors mentioned by Demosthenes, who were visiting the court of Mausolus of Caria. Their warship, falling in with a Greek merchantman from Egypt, carried it to Piraeus, and they kept the prize-money for themselves.

As late as 1818, Captain Beaufort describes the feelings of a caique when a frigate comes in sight. 'Had she been a Turkish man-of-war, they were certain of being pillaged, under the pretext of exacting a present; if a Barbary cruiser, the youngest men would have been forcibly seized for recruits; and even if she had been a Greek merchant ship, their security would have been still precarious; for when one of these large Greek polacres meets even her own countrymen in unfrequented places, she often compels them to assist in loading her, or arbitrarily takes their cargoes at her own price.'

The land too was dangerous, and men in boats were well-advised to remove 'after it grew dark unto another anchorage ... lest observed by day from sea or shore, they might by night be surprised'; and headlands especially had so bad a reputation that the Emperor Julian, who felt strongly about philosophy and disliked the Cynics, compares them to brigands and to those who occupy promontories to damage voyagers.

Such, through the ages, with very short intervals of respite, was the life of the Aegean sailors—resembling that of fish more closely than that of settled landsmen ashore. It would be a sad conclusion that both the men and the fish in the sea are necessarily unhappy. In thinking so one forgets the wide layers of space and time in which their anxieties are packed. To the most harassed sailors in the midst of privation, between one threat and another, the sea gave its golden hours, waking in their eyes that light of many horizons which looks like a smile. There is, in Xenophon's *Hellenica*, the account of a voyage of Iphicrates round the Peloponnesus, with a squadron of galleys. It gives, I think, the atmosphere both of insecurity and leisure, of solitude, adventure, and companionship, the uncertain hazards of every headland, the fleeting safety of every anchorage snatched on a hostile shore.

Iphicrates was the most resourceful of the 4th-century generals of Athens,[5] and revolutionized the warfare of his time by re-arming the light-armed *peltast* of the Thracians, lengthening his spear and sword, and giving him light, easy boots 'still called Iphicratids', and a small, portable shield. When he asked Athens what to do with some gold and ivory statues captured on their way to the shrine at Delphi, he got a cautious government reply not to raise questions about what concerned the gods, but to see that his soldiers were well fed—and so he sold them.

Xenophon, a man who evidently liked picnics and the day to day life of a campaign, described this voyage of Iphicrates with great zest. 'When he began', says Xenophon, 'he went on with all needful preparations for a naval battle as he sailed . . . and, by making his voyage with the oar, he kept his men in better condition of body and caused the ships to go faster. Furthermore, whenever the expedition was going to take the noonday or the evening meal at any particular spot, he

47

would often draw back the head of the column . . . cause the triremes to head towards the land, and start them off at a signal to race towards the shore. It was counted a great prize of victory to be the first to get water or anything else they needed, and the first to get their meal . . . Those who reached the shore last . . . had to put to sea again at the same time as the rest when the signal was given; the result was that those who came in first did everything at their leisure, while those who came in last had to hurry. Again, in setting watches, if he chanced to be taking the midday meal in a hostile country, he posted some on the land, as is proper, but besides he hoisted the masts on the ships and had men keep watch from their tops . . . Further . . . he would not have a fire inside the camp during the night, but kept a light burning in front of his forces, so that no one could approach unobserved. Frequently, however, if it was good weather he would put to sea again immediately after dining . . . Again, when he sailed by day, he would lead the fleet, by signals, at one time in column and at another in line of battle; so that, while still pursuing their voyage they had at the same time practised and become skilled in all the manœuvres of battle before they reached . . . the enemy. And although for the most part they took both their noonday and their evening meals in the enemy's country, nevertheless, by doing only the necessary things, he always got to sea before the enemy's forces arrived to repel him.'

Here, it seems to me, is the very secret of adventure, the solitude, the precariousness, the constant surprise of the Aegean. The life of each hour is taken as a Pandora's box on its own merits, with its troubles and its hopes wrapped within it, with no entanglements of before and after to complicate the clear relation between a man and his days. Who among us, if he has been fortunate enough ever to have enjoyed it, does not remember with delight and longing such a simplified interval of time?

6

COS TO HALICARNASSUS

Captivity

For the deeds of the past are, indeed, an inheritance common to us all; but the ability to make proper use of them . . . is the . . . gift of the wise.
ISOCRATES, Panegyricus, 9.

When we have it in our power to accomplish deeds as lofty as our dreams.
ISOCRATES, Panegyricus, 182.

THE *ELFIN* WAS NOW NEARING, TOWARDS EVENING, THE round towers of the castle of Cos, reflected in the sea. We were in a sadly shrunken channel of traffic, once important, which must have been policed from early days. In remnants and inscriptions the sovereignty of Rhodes still casts her shadow; and the knights of St. John picked it up and held it, in the great trilateral of fortresses that kept the approaches between them—Cos, Rhodes and Halicarnassus (which is now Budrum, from Petrus of the Crusaders).

Having been discouraged by both the shark and Hüseyin in the deeper sea, we were anxious to bathe. *Elfin* stopped; we climbed down her rope ladder and swam towards a sandy beach scattered with pebbles so small and shining that they might have been grey pearls. Willows and fields, and windmills with slow arms turning were beyond, and green hills behind them. A settled look of agriculture and tillage lay over the land. A coastguard boat came out of the town patrolling, saw the red ensign on *Elfin*, gave a glance at the consular party in the water, obviously not officially prepared, and waved amicably as they passed.

Cos to Halicarnassus

In the sunset we strolled through the town, which looks shingled and set by the Italians, its ruins led up to by walks of bougainvillias.   It lies behind its castle and harbour much as it must have done since 366 B.C. when 'the Coans transferred their abode to the city they now inhabit, and made it a notable place.   From this time on its . . . public revenues and private wealth constantly increased . . . so that it became . . . a rival of the leading cities of Greece'.   By the end of the 3rd century it had a standing army of mercenaries; it was the first to organize the later pan-Hellenic festivals, and it was so wealthy that its clubs, together with those of Santorin, improved on the simple garland of leaves with which members were honoured, and beat them out in wreaths of gold.   A sea-fight about 258 B.C., against the fleet of Ptolemy II off Cos, probably inspired the Victory of Samothrace, as she alights on the prow of a galley with such a garland in her hand.

Even before the 4th century and the transfer of the city, the people of Cos were wealthy.   Alcibiades collected booty from them to support his soldiers.   They wove the thread of the wild silkworms of Anatolia before Chinese silks were known, and these and their wines and raisins made them rich.   They built ships and were sailors; in 307 B.C. in the battle off Salamis in Cyprus, Pleistias of Cos was chief pilot to the whole fleet of Demetrius and a man from Halicarnassus commanded the right wing.   They lived easily: a calendar of one of their gymnasia shows eight festivals in a month, over-shadowed by four days of examinations.

There is a materialistic veneer over Cos; bureaucracy, Ptolemaic or Fascist, both alien to the Aegean, seems to have slurred its fine sharp contours.   Ptolemy II was born here (out of wedlock, by the first of the many Ptolemaic Berenices). His palace was built over in Roman times on the same foundations; and the Italians began its restoration in their turn. More than thirty rooms are there, with swimming-pools and atria, mosaic floors, marble walls and pillars—a luxurious vulgarity in which Theocritus[1] remembered his Sicilian hills, though the admirers of Mussolini felt at home. Yet even among these soulless rooms, the modesty of the ancient art flashes out in one gay and exquisite mosaic, quite small. It is a lobster and three fish, done with particles of marble so fine that a modern machine cannot reproduce them.

Here is the careful, naturalistic accurate tradition in which, in the 5th century long before, when the city was still in the hills, Hippocrates laid his enduring foundations and the whole of modern medicine was born. This honesty became the source of scientific induction, from Aristotle to the modern world. The school of Hippocrates flourished through the centuries, in Cos and Alexandria. The Babylonians perhaps first appointed public health officers who were paid a fixed salary and ready to treat all who came, but the Hellenistic doctors, in a direct line from Hippocrates, had a regular tax levied for them, in Egypt, at Halicarnassus, and elsewhere. The pay was meagre—£40 a year is the only salary we hear of—but many decrees have come down to us thanking physicians who made no difference between rich and poor, free and slaves; or worked for nothing during epidemics; or fought the plague in the islands; or, with Xenotimus in Cos, came voluntarily to the city's aid.

As we walked through the welter of civilizations, layer upon layer, that jostle each other in the little town, the moonlight made the poplars bright like waterfalls and the marble seats of a small odeum shone through them. Between pools of shadow the rich light lay on the white stones and raised side-walks—similar to those of modern Calymnos—that cut the agora. It mixed with lamps that shone from cafés, where only a few fishermen now lingered; and lay warm and soft on the decks of caiques pulling at their hawsers by the quay; and on the castle towers in the water, where a shadowy gate was roofed with shafts of horizontal columns, green stone carried from Halicarnassus over the bay.

The two great fortresses are in sight of each other across the water. There must have been intercourse between the harbours, Dorians of the island mingling with mainland Carians long before the first historical queen, with Carian father and Cretan mother, led Greeks of Halicarnassus, Cos, Nisyrus and Calynda in five ships under Xerxes to the Persian war.[2]

A queen who rules suggests 'barbarian' influences of matriarchy, presumable among Carians and known to have existed among Lycians farther south. A mixed atmosphere is noticeable all down this Anatolian seaboard where none of the cities had joined the Delian League in its early days.[3] The tolerance of Herodotus was reared there, and, in Halicarnassus his native city, the Greek and barbarian fusion—the single world of Alexander's dream—was already in a small way accomplished. It was a Greek capital for Carian kings, spread like an open fan round its bay.

At its eastern end the acropolis, which was then an island with castle and arsenal upon it, hid a secret port screened by high walls: from here the second Artemisia surprised a fleet of Rhodians in the harbour. The palace of King Mausolus stood west of it, at the water's edge, and from it a wide street led below the agora round the curve of the bay to the western end of the town.

Here the walls, still visible, came down a slope from the temple of Hermes and Aphrodite, where the fountain Salmacis was supposed to make hermaphrodites of those who drank.[4] We looked for this fountain, whose waters D. B. was prepared to experiment with in a prudent way: but we could not find it, and it may have deviated, since Captain Beaufort only mentions a warm subterranean stream that flows from a cave into the sea from the north-east of a little island nearby. He found Budrum 'a snug port, frequented by the small Turkish cruisers'.

Budrum Castle

Under the two summits of a second, northern acropolis, the ruins of the temple of Mars were seen by Leake in 1800, and by Newton later, who managed, after nearly three years of rough life on the coast of Asia Minor, to send home three hundred and eighty-four cases of antiques. Inside them were twelve slabs from the mausoleum, extracted from the walls of the Knights' castle through the influence of Stratford Canning in Istanbul.

It was no easy matter, even in the early days of this century, to get into the castle. A French enthusiast, mentioned by Captain Beaufort in 1818, obtained a paper, but the local pasha pointed out to him that the permit specified entry and not exit, and the Frenchman thought it wiser to desist. Newton, in the middle of the century, found that the long brass guns of the Knights still armed the batteries, and their powder lay caked up in the magazines; and the cistern would have been in use if a soldier had not fallen in and been drowned in it a few years before, since when, and instead of fishing him out, they 'ceased to use the water'. In the early 1900's, a friend of mine found the place crowded with Albanian prisoners, who used to make little baskets and toys and sell them at the gate.

The castle superseded the ancient city. It swallowed the mausoleum, the world's wonder, to whose building the widowed queen Artemisia had called the best artists of Greece; only fragments remained—the frieze and a horse of the great quadriga, the work of Pythios, found by Newton and dragged by eighty men to be shipped to England; and Mausolus himself, in the British Museum, larger than life. While the pasha's caique was held by contrary winds in harbour, the lions from the castle court were shipped at the eleventh hour, the colours of their painted bodies and scarlet tongues fading as they travelled. The green basement, the monumental stairway, the mouldings painted red on a blue ground, had long before been cracked and used as stone, and the white columns sliced and carved with feudal coats of arms. Nothing now remains but a flat ground, ploughed and planted with fig trees among the houses, where the great erection stood in the middle of the town, above the corniche road that skirts the bay.

It was new when Alexander's Macedonians burnt the city. The Christians saw it in A.D. 1406, though damaged by earthquakes. Then Schlegelholt, one of the German Knights, undertook to build a fortress, and used certain steps of white marble which stood, in the form of a stone staircase, in the middle of a field near the harbour. After a few days' work, the men noticed an aperture, and by it they entered a large square hall embellished with marble columns, their bases, capitals, architraves, friezes and cornices carved in demi-relief . . . 'which having admired closely, and after having considered in their imagination the singularity of the work, at last they pulled down, cracked and broke up to use as they had done the rest'. Through another low door, they found, in another hall, a sepulchre with a vase of white marble, very beautiful and shining marvellously, which, for lack of sufficient time, they did not disturb, as the retreat had just sounded. The next day they returned, too late, for the ground was strewn all around with little pieces of cloth of gold and spangles of the same metal. This is the story, as it is given on the authority of d'Alechamps, the editor of Pliny, who heard it from the Commander de la Tourette, a Lyonese Knight present at Budrum at the time.[5] And after all this destruction, the new fortress offered no resistance and surrendered to Suleiman the First.

When we sailed from Cos to Budrum (Halicarnassus) in the morning, the Ceramic gulf lay under a *bonaccia* that made it pale and smooth as sky. At the quayside, under the western castle wall, a caique was loading figs; their dusty oatmeal-coloured bags were being fitted between stays in the open hold. The few Turkish sponge-fishers mostly come from here and so do the best of the Turkish tangerines. The five thousand

The Kaymakam

inhabitants live quietly as mice in little houses in gardens, and a fortnightly coasting steamer unites them with Istanbul, Smyrna, or the south. In one of their courts, crowded with vines and flowers and paved with rounded pebbles set in patterns, the *Kaymakam* invited us to breakfast at a small table covered with dishes of jams and clotted creams and biscuits, a blue convolvulus beside each plate. He was a young man, here for two years or three. A badge of the Political Science School was in his buttonhole, and he had the quiet manner of the men who now manage Turkey, more ready for action than words. His fancy went to clothes—a surrealist tie and bright blue suit with a white lattice pattern, and hat inclining to a panama: this gaiety is a benefit brought back by America to Turkey, and may, if encouraged, counter-act at least in colour the dreary monotony which Atatürk took from us in the West. I have seen a young man, on the first day of Bairam, walking down the street in a turquoise coat and dove-grey trousers, with primrose leather shoes, and hoped that he foreshadowed a pleasing and promising return towards the brightness which all the early travellers admired.

The *Kaymakam* and D. B. went about their business, and I spent the morning in the castle. I walked unhindered through open gates that led across the moat to a curtain and inner curtain, by a fountain carved with St. George to the well of the drowned soldier, and the chapel with Byzantine shape and Gothic door and windows. Towers were scattered here and there over the top of the rock, built by the various nations; their escutcheons, carved from sliced shafts of pillars, were let into the walls near blocks of green stone or column from the mausoleum. On the south-east tower, over a more ancient lion crouching on a bracket, the Plantagenet arms were carved for Edward IV and his nobles; the names of Sir Thomas Sheffield, 1514, and John Kendal, a Turcopalier of 1477–1500, were somewhere about, seen by Newton.

Over the deserted walls, on the disused steps, a feeling of intimacy hovered, a touch that once spoke of home to the crusader and could still be recognized:

> Salva nos domine vigilantes
> Custode nos dormientes
> Nisi dominus costodieret civitatem
> Frustra vigilet qui custodit eam

was written in bad but heartfelt Latin above a western door.

The goats pushed their hard little worn hooves into places where stones had fallen, and followed the joints of the walls, and cropped the roots that grew in them, and kept the ruins clean. The sea below lay smooth under fanning ripples that moved without breaking its surface. In its transparent depth, in shafts of sun, fish browsed at the castle foundations, investigating them head-on with dull curiosity intent on food. The grass-grown fosse itself seemed like a pool—not free in a universal way as Greek ruins are free, but as if Time had been trapped there, and grown clogged and stagnant, and remained. Nothing of what the castle had been built for counted in it any longer; its language was intelligible to me because it was the language of my people, with few centuries between us; but compared with the idylls of Theocritus, the work of the Knights here was dust.

Ionian honesty

They too constructed their present, and hacked and destroyed a past to build a dream of such courage that the world of their own age vanished around them, and the world of their promise alone was truly alive. There was no fault in the dream: it was the fosse, the long windowless enclosure, that gave it the feeling of a prison—walls which keep the unbeliever out, which kill Socrates, and confine the spirit whose only home is its immortal freedom.

Theocritus saw his simple landscape in its own colours and it excluded no one and lives for ever. So does Hippocrates and his school, and Aristotle when he followed in their footsteps—looking at the object before him directly, nor wavering towards the fashions of his day. Sometimes he wavers and when he does so the whole science of astronomy goes back for two thousand years. The Ionian honesty shines more purely with Theophrastus, who was born in Lesbos, the son of a fuller, and followed Aristotle as head of the Lyceum: whose botany, nourished by the scientists of Alexander's armies, has scarcely yet been superseded; and who, studying the ways of animals with insight and affection, came to the conclusion that they are not separated from us by any definite boundary. He leaned out over the world as if it were his window-sill, and wrote down what he saw—placing his objects near or far, but always uncircumscribed, so that their distances were merely distance, cut off by no human wall.

So we too look into our past, treating it as far as we can with respect for its own sake, because of the scattered fragments of truth it must contain. With infinite consideration, with ceaseless care, we disentangle them, and try to keep them intact in their integrity, as free, as far as we can make them, from the twist of our own time and of ourselves—never forgetting that somewhere in that knot is the beginning of a thread that we must follow, on whose right choice the future of all must depend.

7

CNIDUS

The Persian Government

Nicomedes, King of Bythynia, offered to redeem the whole public debt of Cnidus in exchange for Praxiteles' Aphrodite. Quoted by NEWTON from PLINY.

There was Temnus . . . not a large city . . . and Aegae, and other places in which people were able to dwell without being subject to the King.
XENOPHON, Hellenica, IV, 8, 5.

THE MOUNTAIN RANGE OF CNIDUS, ALMOST SUBMERGED, stretches to a thin promontory as if it were a spear levelled against the sunset. Its northern slopes plunge steeply, almost without villages, without roads or shelter, into the deep Ceramic gulf. There is easier land on the south; but even there a single road ends half-way along the prong at Datcha, villages thin out, and Yazi Köy, the last of them, is two and a half hours from the tip, and harvests its meagre fields there from that distance.

The promontory took its name from the Triopian Apollo, whose temple was probably some miles inland. At its very end a small headland, once an island, was called Chersonnesus, joined to the mainland city by a bridge; its inhabitants dedicated their offerings at Olympia separately from the rest of Cnidus, 'as if a suburb of Ephesus dedicated separately from the town', Pausanias rather bitingly remarks.

On the west, the island broke in striated cliffs, and caught the violence of the Aegean; but towards the land it sloped like a theatre, to the bridge which is now an isthmus between the harbours, and towards the main city of Cnidus on the slope opposite,[1] 'the mainland of Caria where are their most noteworthy possessions'. Foundations show there, of terraces and walls and temples. An east-west street ran below a theatre whose piers are standing, to the temple of Demeter under a cliff where stone was quarried; a Corinthian temple and Doric portico were seen by Newton on the western hillside, and a small Doric temple on the shore of the trireme harbour. A road climbed to the north gate, and the agora lay below. But the sites of the sanctuaries of Aphrodite, whom the Cnidians held in very great honour, are undiscovered and possibly belong also to the older Cnidus inland—Doritis the Bountiful, the oldest; Acraea of the Height; and the newest, called the Cnidian by men generally, but Euploia, or Fair Voyage, by the Cnidians themselves. These places remained in Conon's mind when he won his victory and returned to the Piraeus, and he too built a temple to Aphrodite, in memory of Cnidus.[2]

Lucian, who probably visited the Aphrodite temple, found it small, with an entrance at either end, under shady trees. In it the statue stood, the portrait of Phryne, and under it an inscription added by someone who put his shabby mind into the mouth of the goddess:

'When Cypris saw Cypris at Cnidus, "Alas," said she: "Where did Praxiteles see me naked?"' Praxiteles' own inscription was carved in the theatre on the base of the statue of Eros and was free from such later prudery. "Taking his heart for the pattern"—he begins as Sir Philip Sidney might have done—"Praxiteles portrayed the love he felt; and gave me to Phryne as the price of love, myself. So the spell I cast, comes no longer from my bow, but from the eyes of another."[3]

At the time when this work was ordered, Cos too commissioned from Praxiteles a clothed Aphrodite, whose success was not equal to that of the naked Phryne, and indeed the city fell into debt and was unable to pay. Both are lost; but out of the sea last year, entangled in a fisherman's net, between Cos and Cnidus, a bronze head was rescued, in whose beauty the age of Praxiteles is echoed. The veil has been eaten and encrusted by the water; the metal has broken away where the rise of the breasts begins; but the face is intact. It is not like any other Greek head that I know: it has the long, bony oval of the Mediterranean, and curved nose and features that promise to be fine in age. There is the quality of a Renaissance Madonna, a compassion rare in the ancient world; and this sentiment is wrought with delicacy not in but through the features, so that the goddess expresses a pity beyond human pity—and yet is aloof and not involved. She is in the museum of Smyrna, shut in a cage of glass—a sad degradation for beauty that should need no other than itself to protect it. Whether it was the sight of it so captive; or the presence of the unattainable which perhaps the fingers of the sculptor felt without his knowledge; or mere loveliness, rising for the comfort of men from her deep bays, I cannot tell; but I stood rooted and speechless before the statue from the sea.

The tip of the peninsula and the island, united by their mole, almost made Cnidus a double city, for a great part of the inhabitants lived on the island, which sheltered the two harbours. Steps, and the ends of store-rooms quarried in the rock are visible along them, and their oval basins, one greater and one smaller, lie side by side. The northern is shallow now, that held twenty warships in Strabo's day; but the southern is still protected by the foundations and short stretches of moles that ran towards each other from east and west nearly a hundred feet down on the sand below.[4]

We twice visited Cnidus, and made for this shelter when, on our second voyage, we fought our way in bad weather along the northern shore. The wind was crossing low passes behind us, and blowing the sea into fans of spray beyond a coastal strip of calm which we were hugging, and Hüseyin's successor, an old man fond of the harbour cafés, looked miserable at the wheel.

"He wants us to go back to Budrum," D. B. shouted. "Shall we do it or risk and get round the cape if we can?"

Influenced—if the truth must be told—by Strabo's twenty ships in the nearest harbour, and unaware of its silting, I said what D. B. obviously meant me to say, and we ventured, and the sea was kind. The sun came out. The waves moved round the bright Triopian cliffs solid and dark as night but with unbroken ridges; and the *Elfin* swung her little mast aslant against the great headland of the sun-god, and reached the southern harbour. There we could watch the restless horizon tossing where the mole of the Cnidians sank to huge and shapeless blocks of its foundations under water, and saved us from all but a short surface movement of the sea.

As the evening deepened, four stray fishing caiques also dropped in to shelter. They sent a lobster as a present for our supper, and moved off before the dawn. They looked humble in the great historic scene; their crews, with heads wrapped up in woollen caps and scarves, carried saddle-bags (*heybes*) to a little cave, where they lit a fire and slept warm.

But in 1952, on our first visit, a summer afternoon lay on the resting water and we slid from Budrum easily, in four hours instead of six and a half, along the steep dry hills, to the northern harbour, where two round towers must once have held a chain. They were neatly and sharply defined in the clear air, like those careful drawings made by young clergymen and squires, travelling a hundred years ago or more in the footprints of the classics or the apostles: they gave the topsy-turvy feeling, so common in the Levant, that the landscape is being copied out of books.

One tower was half in ruins, but the other was intact, with its chisel-marks clear upon it, at the end of a wall that climbed the Triopian headland. A lighthouse, like a small white church, stood steep above it; a domed imamzadé and two hovels were on the mainland below, inhabited by a shepherd and three soldiers. All the rest belonged to the ancient world, great lines of foundations, honey-coloured blocks, that still give a city feeling to the fierce and empty promontory. Above the town, north of the theatre, one could see three hairpin bends of the ancient chariot way propped on blocks of polygonal wall. The chariots could almost drive there now if the rubble were removed.

High above, on the ridge of the hill, coloured like rock, the top of Cnidus fortress showed. Many centuries of skill and fashion went to make it—from polygonal to smooth neat rectangular stone. We climbed by its northern, less ruined side, whose approaches—facing the land—were held by a chain of square towers of fine Hellenistic workmanship; a twenty-foot height of wall still remains to join them here and there.

From this elevation, scented with rosemary and myrtle and the pungent hillside bushes, the Cnidian sentinels saw all that went on below. They saw the harbours like twin lakes, and the Odeum with its marble seats, beside the promenade along the shore. They looked down as if from the air on streets that ran between the terraced houses; on the precinct of Demeter, where the trees grew as they grow now that there is no building to be shaded; and somewhere in the eastern landscape they saw perhaps the Triopian temple, where the six Dorian cities held their games and gave brazen cauldrons to the victors, until a competitor from Halicarnassus cheated by keeping the prize for himself instead of dedicating it to the temple, and Halicarnassus was disqualified and the six cities reduced to five. On the edges of the harbours they saw the moles busy with people, clearer than I could see their ruin, though that showed plainly enough through the clear water from this height. And beyond the promontory, they could look out at islands—Telos, where Telines, the ancestor of Gelon came from, and took the Triopian rites to Sicily;[5] Nisyros, the home of Nireus, most beautiful of the Greeks except Achilles, who set out with three ships for Troy;[6] and Syme and Rhodes in the south. The sea is like a polished corridor between them, so smooth and narrow, so obviously meant for traffic.

In 412 B.C., after Sicily, Cnidus like Chios revolted from the Athenians at the instigation of the Persian governor, Tissaphernes. Twelve ships from Sparta and her allies, coming to help him there, left half their squadron on guard and with the rest cruised round Triopium to seize any merchantmen sailing from Egypt. The capital, at that time, was still on the ancient site, towards the middle of the peninsula, and the Triopian cape stood probably as lonely as today; the six Peloponnesian cruisers were seized by Athenians from Samos, though the crews escaped overland, to help in a successful defence of their city.[7]

A second Spartan fleet of twenty-seven ships took a southern route for greater security and reached Caunus. Feeling safe there, in Persian territory, they sent a message through Caria to the Spartans at Miletus, asking for a convoy along the coast.

The new arrivals had eleven government commissioners on board, empowered to look into the conduct of the admiral in Miletus, and to supersede him if necessary. He came hurrying down the coast towards them, sacking the unfortunate

Cos, already devastated by earthquake, on his way, and reached Cnidus by night. Here the citizens told him to sail straight on and catch the Athenians, who were cruising south of the Triopian headland off Syme and Rhodes, on the look-out for the twenty-seven ships; and he came upon them straggling in the darkness, and chased them to Halicarnassus after an untidy battle; then he and the twenty-seven from Caunus sailed all together, and set up a trophy in Syme.

They returned to anchor in Cnidus where, meanwhile, the latent trouble between the Spartans and Persians had come to a head. This trouble, with the Persian–Greek relations that lay behind it, must be investigated.

Tissaphernes and Pharnabazus, the governors of the coast-lands, were the men who dealt with the Greeks of that time; and the Greek histories, written by their enemies, have left portraits often unfair and always incomplete.

Tissaphernes in two treaties with Spartan admirals, had seen that the Persian King's right to all country ruled by his ancestors was recognized. The eleven commissioners noticed that this gave him back the northern mainland of Greece together with the coasts and islands of Asia, and rejected the treaties; and Tissaphernes went off in a rage. He lived in Caria, where the Persian interest was stronger than in Ionia; and he had quelled a revolt there, and been given the governor-ship of the three maritime provinces, Caria, Ionia and Lydia, as a reward. His policy with the Greeks was to keep both sides underpaid and weak—a policy attributed to Alcibiades' advice, but which anyone on the spot could think out for himself. It was less damaging to Greece than the whole-hearted support of Sparta which Cyrus, when he came, carried in his instructions from the Persian court, and which could be trusted, in time and because of Sparta's incapacity at sea, to clear away the main-land Greeks from the shores of Asia.

In 407 B.C. Cyrus came, Tissaphernes was superseded as

Tissaphernes and Cyrus

Commander in Chief and governor of Lydia, and friendship with Sparta became the Persian order of the day. Cyrus was the King's brother and Tissaphernes warned the Persian court that he was collecting troops against them; he no doubt disliked Cyrus, but his loyalty to the kings who had exalted his house and married into his family must also have counted together with the Persians' love for their kings, which has run in a clear streak right through their history.

Tissaphernes at all events became the hero of the battle of Cunaxa where Cyrus was killed. It was he who threw his cavalry into the gap between the Ten Thousand and the Persians in Cyrus' army, and sealed the day; it was he who pursued the Ten Thousand up to the Kurdish border at Jazira and who—whether or no by the King's order—betrayed the Grecian generals in his tent. Xenophon and Plutarch have given him a bad press between them, but the 'abandoned character' is a normal European description of the hardness of Asia, where cruelty—when the luck turns—becomes an obedience, an alignment with fate if religious or dynastic loyalties support it. It would no doubt be a better world if more of its inhabitants minded about murder; but there is no reason to think that Tissaphernes did not try now and then to do what he could for his friends. Alcibiades escaped from his prison, and that is difficult in the East against the will of one's captor.

However this may be, Tissaphernes came back from the war triumphant to his former provinces in Asia. Athens was out of the ring, and Lysander had his eye on the riches of Ionia; and the Ten Thousand had reappeared in Asia Minor, and saw in the Persian governor only an enemy of Cyrus who had been their friend. In the background, the vengeance of Cyrus' mother hung like a Damocles sword above his head. In this atmosphere, in 396 B.C., the Spartan expedition under King Agesilaus set sail against him. It began with a sacrifice at Aulis in the steps of Agamemnon, and was a rehearsal for

Alexander. To a legally constituted Persian governor it was, and must have looked like, an unjustified attack.

Plutarch is very smug, and describes Agesilaus making a feint into Caria 'to revenge Tissaphernes' perfidy by an artifice which justice recommended', and then turning into the neighbouring province of Phrygia where he had no quarrel at all. Here he made himself master of immense treasure, and 'showed his friends that to deceive an enemy is not only just but glorious, and the way to add profit to pleasure'. In earlier years, Tissaphernes had been sufficiently popular with the Ephesians to defend their temple with them against an Athenian assault: but now Agesilaus in Ephesus, pointing to the soft white bodies of naked prisoners and to the rich spoil heaped beside them, said to his men: "Those are the men you fight, and this is what you fight for." A few years before, Athens had invented, as a new punishment, exclusion from the Hellespont or Ionia; and Lysander had collected over a thousand talents after Aegospotami: the west of Asia was too rich to be left alone. And now, 'in consequence of their success' says Plutarch, 'the Spartans could pillage the King's country in full security, and had the satisfaction of seeing Tissaphernes properly punished', for the King rewarded his defeat by sending Tithraustes to supersede him and cut off his head.

*　　*　　*　　*

If Tissaphernes had a case against the mainland Greeks, his Phrygian neighbour Pharnabazus had a better. His family had lived the life of country gentlemen ever since Xerxes gave lands to their ancestor nearly a century before. Surrounded by excellent cavalry, they had governed from father to son, in their palace of Dascyleium on the Black Sea coast, with large villages round about stored with provisions, and wild animals in enclosed parks or open spaces. There was also a river, full of all kinds of fish, flowing by the palace, and winged game in abundance for those who knew how to take it. There, in

413, when the news of Sicily came, Pharnabazus could find messengers for Sparta among the Greek exiles who were his guests; and sent them to treat separately from those of Tissaphernes, hoping to get at the tribute of the coastal cities before him. And when the Spartan fleet, unpaid and miserable in the south, finally moved towards him, and was weather-bound at Delos, he was able to convey the commander safely through the Aeolian and Mysian lands. There was, in fact, a settled and friendly atmosphere about the government of Pharnabazus.

He helped the Spartans, and gathered their fugitives during the last Athenian flicker of victory, and comforted them for the loss of their ships. 'There was plenty of timber in the King's land—so long as their bodies were safe,' he said, and gave each man a cloak and subsistence for two months, and set the cities to rebuild the ships they had lost. Everything one hears of him is pleasant. Though an ally of Sparta, yet when Lysander's thugs in Miletus in 405 put the popular party to the sword, and the most respectable citizens fled to him, he received them kindly and, giving each of them a pound or so, settled them in a fortress in Lydia.* He cannot have liked to see the way in which the worst minorities were forced on cities of Asia inhabited by his acquaintance and friends; and after the Spartan victory, when Lysander expected to plunder the lands freely, Pharnabazus complained, and had him recalled.

But in less than ten years the political circle revolved and Sparta and Persia were at war. The Ten Thousand under Dercyllidas were moving in and out of the cities of Aeolis, and in 397 B.C. Pharnabazus was in Caria, where Tissaphernes was general in chief, to assure him that he was ready to make war to drive the Greeks out of the territory of the King. In 396 Agesilaus came out, and the gentlemanly truces with which Dercyllidas had conducted the Asiatic war were ended;

* This must have been Tissaphernes, since the refugees were settled in Lydia and not in Phrygia.

Pharnabazus with his camp-animals and baggage, his drinking cups and other valuables, was reduced to make first for one and then for another part of the country, like a nomad concealing his encampments for fear of being surrounded.

The Spartan King spent a winter near Dascyleium, whose hunting and fishing amenities Xenophon so much admired; and Pharnabazus attacked his own grounds with two scythe-bearing chariots and his horsemen behind him.

When the winter was nearly over, a Greek friend from Cyzicus nearby arranged a meeting with the Spartan King. Xenophon, surely an eye-witness, describes it, in a grassy place where the thirty Spartans were lying on the ground. Pharnabazus came, in a fine dress, and his attendants began to spread rugs for him, but he too lay on the ground without further ado, and held out his right hand; and Agesilaus held out his to meet it. After this Pharnabazus began to speak, for he was the elder:

"Agesilaus, and all you Lacedaemonians who are present, I became your friend and ally at the time when you were at war with the Athenians, and not only did I make your fleet strong by providing money, but on the land I myself fought on horse-back with you and drove your enemies into the sea . . . And now I am brought to such a pass by you that I have not so much as a meal in my own land unless, like the beasts, I pick up a bit of what you may leave. And the beautiful dwellings and parks . . . which my father left me, in which I took delight . . . I see cut down, all these dwellings burned to the ground. If it is that I do not understand either what is righteous or what is just, do you teach me how these are the deeds of men who know how to repay favours."

Thus he spoke, and the thirty Spartans were filled with shame and fell silent, until at last Agesilaus answered, and said the best he could, how glad he would be to see Pharnabazus their friend: and promised that in any case he would leave his land as speedily as he could (as Xenophon remarks, the spring was almost at hand), and "even if war continues, we shall withhold our hands from you and yours, so long as we can turn our attack against another".

With these words he broke up the meeting. And Pharnabazus mounted his horse and rode away, but his son, remaining behind, ran up to Agesilaus and said to him:

"Agesilaus, I make you my guest-friend." And immediately he gave his javelin—it was a beautiful one—to Agesilaus. And he, accepting it, took off and gave to the boy in return a splendid trapping which his secretary had round his horse's neck. Then the boy leaped upon his horse and followed after his father.

So we leave them—though we meet Pharnabazus again, and this time with Conon and the Athenians in the south. But meanwhile, from such stray glimpses, we may guess at the Persian side of the question in Asia. We see that reduced to its essentials, the Persian idea was tribute and not dominion. If the King got his revenue, the coastal governors lived in comparative security and ease; if the governors could collect the tribute without interfering in the complications of Greek city-politics, they were satisfied to do so; and the governors themselves, in their northern and southern provinces, had interests and vanities sufficiently far apart for a clever Greek to manage when he wished.

The 'liberty' of the cities of Asia never seemed to be a great difficulty to the Persian mind. "If you are willing to make a truce until I can send to the King, I think you could accomplish this object," says Tissaphernes to Agesilaus, and probably meant it; for the tribute, which he cared about, was a separate matter —was not held (by either side) to be an infraction of civic independence. 'He undertook,' says Plutarch of Tissaphernes, 'that the king would leave the Grecian cities to be governed by their own laws.' And when Tissaphernes had been done away with, Tithraustes his successor—in a letter which Xenophon must have seen—confirmed the point of view. 'The King,' it ran, 'deems it fitting that you should sail back home, and that the cities in Asia, *retaining their independence, should render him their ancient tribute.*'

As for the cities, they carried, through many centuries, one single and masterful desire—and that was for autonomy as understood by the city state. The mere word, in pathetic unreality, evoked enthusiasms, wreaths and dedications, long after the substance had vanished. The sentiment was strong enough to impose itself not only on the acts but on the feelings of Alexander and his successors; it cast a fleeting illusion of gentleness over the first approach of Rome. We meet it everywhere through the 4th century B.C. in the pages of orators and historians. It explains, I think, the apparent fickleness of the cities of Asia: they were constantly turning towards powers that promised them the one thing they longed for, and every power, forced by stronger necessities, deceived them in turn. The trust in Athens faded, as the confederacy turned to empire: as early as 427 B.C. Ionian and Lesbian exiles urged the Spartans to seize one of the Aeolic cities or the town of Cyme, as a base for effecting the revolt of Ionia.[8] After Sicily the Milesians, with Tissaphernes and his cavalry, showed great ardour for the war against the Athenians—until a year later—when they surprised the fort built by Tissaphernes in Miletus and turned out the garrison and caused Lichas, the chairman of the eleven Spartan commissioners, to say that the Milesians and the rest in the King's country ought to show a reasonable submission to Tissaphernes and to pay him court, until the war should be happily settled! The Milesians were angry with him for this and for other things of the kind, and, upon his dying of sickness, would not allow him to be buried where the Spartans desired. The same see-saw happened in Cnidus, which revolted at the instigation of Tissaphernes, and had expelled his garrison by the following year; and in Ephesus, where the history of Thucydides breaks off with Tissaphernes offering sacrifice to Artemis, who was good for both Greek and Barbarian alike.

Autonomy, the cities' desire, was one of those words that are like the apple of discord itself. It meant democracy to Athens, oligarchy to Sparta, to Persia the paying of tribute, to the cities the wish to be left alone or helped in their own way through the terrible divisions that opened their gates to perennial massacre. It brought the continual surprise of one party by another. In the revolt of Chios, the mass of the Chians were not privy to the negotiations. The many were amazed and confounded, while the few had so arranged that the council should be sitting at the time, so as to vote in their favour. The same thing happened in Rhodes, when the eleven Spartan commissioners sailed from Cnidus and put through an oligarchic revolution, to the great alarm of the mass of the inhabitants who were not privy to the intrigue. Through century after century the story was repeated. Autonomy might have been attained, but the class division, which cut in a horizontal way across the Grecian world, destroyed it. 'In all the cities,' the orator says to the Athenians, 'the people is your friend, and either does not revolt with the oligarchy, or, if forced to do so, becomes at once the enemy of the insurgents; so that you have the masses on your side . . .'[9]

Mutilated as it was, the hope of autonomy persisted through all the centuries. It remained the first of the cities' desires, and, two hundred and thirty years later, when the wars of Alexander were over, it inspired Lampsacus and Smyrna in their first appeal to Rome. Thucydides puts the truth into the mouth of Phrynichus in Samos. "The cities never prefer servitude, with an oligarchy or a democracy," says he, "to freedom with the constitution they actually enjoy, to whichever type it belongs. . . ." No sooner did they get a moderate government and liberty of action, than they went on to absolute freedom.

Left alone with Persia, a compromise might have been achieved, a measure of independence reconcilable with tribute. It was not impossible. The rich cities of Phoenicia, Heraclea and Byzantium in the north, or Rhodes in the south, showed that autonomy could pay; the Persians were unwilling to disturb their flow of revenues by war. But the mainland of Greece, like a stronger planet, drew Asia from its orbit. Conon with his eight ships in the Rhodian sea will once more swing the Aegean to the west. In sight of his battlefield, in Cnidus, one may think of the 'freedom' of the cities of Asia, the unattainable that meant so much. The memory of it came from days when inland places were far away from these long promontories, and the coast had room for all. Boats could set out with their rowers and find a headland and build a city and stay. Freedom to sit on the stone seats of one's council, and see all the citizens together, and come to a decision of one's own! It is still in the air of Cnidus.

As I came down from the causeway through the theatre, a black snake like a shy god slid into the laurel thicket; I stepped over the stones rattled by earthquakes on their foundations, and climbed from terrace to terrace of corn where the peasants build shallow walls round the pockets of the ancient houses. The full ears, ready for harvest, beat their slight weight against my passing hand, as if they too would spend their weak resistance for the headland's warm and living peace. So remote, so undisturbed was the great hollow, that its own particular divinity seemed to fill it—complete in being as a cup is filled to its brim. There was no judgment here, but only consequence of actions; the good corn filled itself out in deeper places and the bad dwindled among stones, and all things were a part of each other in a soil that someone's building two thousand or more years ago had fattened or spoiled. A fair-haired woman, still beautiful, with green eyes, was reaping. I asked if I might photograph, and she called her husband, who came climbing up and stood beside her, and glanced at her and smiled when I said she was like the English to look at: they were both pleased by her fairness, and there was a happy friendliness between them. He had the oval face of the Mediterranean, and she the straight northern brows: and the history of the world had washed over Cnidus to produce them both, from the days when their ancestors, in the oldest city of the peninsula, joined in building the Hellenium in Egypt, or sent the first caryatid to Delphi.[10]

They had travelled many stages—colonizing Lipara, or rowing Gillus to Tarentum across the scarce-known West. The most celebrated astronomer of the early 4th century was Eudoxus of Cnidus; the man who warned Julius Caesar of his danger on the Ides of March was Artemidorus, a rhetorician from Cnidus. The city came into the great orbit of Rhodes; it lost its freedom, turning away from Rome to Mithridates; the Cilician pirates sacked it. The Roman peace then came, and the world seemed safe; the stoas, the temples, the three theatres increased their ancient splendours; the city continued to blossom on its long stalk of land like a flower in the brightness of the sea.

Living there from day to day, from year to year, from century to century, one might scarcely notice that the voice of a people had become merely municipal. Yet the dream persisted; the little cities were drowning in a larger unity, and every bough they clutched broke in their hand; yet the ardour with which they clutched can be seen by the waves of enthusiasm for anything that seemed to give this freedom, for Pergamum, Rome, Antiochus, Mithridates—and the waves of disappointment that followed. Gradually the darkness closes. The boulders of the hill beneath its forts roll down on the causeway of Cnidus; ships come to take away the marble columns; they build a palace in Egypt for Muhammad Ali. Half a century later, in 1857, Newton camps there, in eight Crimean huts, among jackals and wolves and pirates; and finds the anchorage dangerous in winter and Cape Crio very difficult for small craft to double in bad weather. Above a deep cliff inlet, south of the track where the ancient tombs stand for miles on their square foundations, he found better shelter; and the road his sailors made is as he left it, dropping into the deep water at a convenient place for the lowering of the marble lion with red tongue that he lifted from its mausoleum—the monument, as he thought it, of Conon's victory there in sight.

It is wrecked now: its pyramid roof, its engaged Doric columns, lie shapeless; as soon as he sailed, the peasants must have pulled it to pieces, hoping for treasure. The desolation continues. What government could prevent it in such loneliness?

As I walked down, along the quayside of the southern harbour, beside the Odeum in the dusk, I saw a wall of loose stones that seemed to shine with a strange transparency: when I came near, I discovered it to be built of marble, pieces of cornice, fragments of ornament, their edges sharp and brittle from the newness of the cutting; and in the long grass behind, propped up to make a boundary, a metope showed three figures and an urn washing away in the rains.

When Mehmet had given us our supper in the cabin of *Elfin*, we climbed into the dinghy and rowed about the southern harbour under the full moon. Three of the three hundred fishing caiques of Budrum were there beside us, the day's catch of sponges spread out on the cut stone quayside of Triopium. The boats themselves squatted dark in the headland shadow, their rough and tattered sailors all asleep. A haunted, a magical remoteness lay on the sleeping town; the tiers of its streets, the great conglomerate blocks of its foundations still looked in the night like darkened gold; the grey wall of the high sky-

The days of Cnidus

line and the hillside it was cut from melted, as if into their element, unseen into the sky. Only the water was awake, motionless but filled with shafts of moonlight—a warm yellow light that sank through layer upon layer, through depth upon depth to reach and gild the sand. These shafts of light, fluid in the mystery around them, seemed to me like the days of Cnidus—the few known, the infinite number unknown.

As we drifted, looking for the mole, the moonlight under water crossed like swords, like wavering veils, like phantoms—like all the events and dreams: and suddenly, with a strange emotion, we saw very far down yet clear in the moonlit depth the pavement of the mole's foundations, a broad causeway of blocks gnawed by the sea for more than two thousand years, laid there with pride and toil when the Cnidians still trusted their freedom and the city was young.

8

THE DORIC PENINSULA

Decadence or Transition

The general, I may say liberal, instructions of the admiralty, left me no doubts of their approbation, however I should employ my time; whether in effecting a mere survey of the coast or in the investigation of the geography and antiquities of the adjacent countries.

F. BEAUFORT, Karamania, 270.

And you have fallen into such a practice, not because your natures are inferior to your ancestors, but because they were in a condition to think highly of themselves, while from you, Men of Athens, this power is taken away.

DEMOSTHENES, On the duties of the State.

WE LEFT ABOUT NOON NEXT DAY, AFTER A BATHE IN THE harbour in the sun, and nosed along the south coast, fishing in the loneliness of Caria. It was done with a line that trailed a bit of metal which no fish seemed to appreciate, and which caught continually on the sea-floor. Everyone enjoyed it. D. B. sat on deck or vaulted from side to side, winding or unwinding his coil with moments of drama; Hüseyin kept one eye on the wheel and one on the rocks close by, and rowed the dinghy patiently at intervals to disentangle the hook from the seaweed; and Mehmet stood at the prow in his white cooking apron to look for shoals ahead. The peninsula sloped down with rust-coloured hills like paws of sphinxes; they were clothed with the thankless burnet—*Potirium spinosum*—spiky cushions yellow now in autumn, as if the iron seeping through this soil had run into their veins. The gentle Ionia had vanished; the cliffs hung sheer, with pine trees here and there, with pink or white streaks in tightly-packed strata over caves, and overhangs filled with the nests of doves.

Somewhere out of sight ran the track that was once the main road to Cnidus, where Newton found a corbelled bridge and a fortress with polygonal walls and gate intact on a hill; the road, he says, could be traced for six miles or so by the tombs beside it, to Yazi Köy and a medieval castle. I had not read either Newton's or J. Cook's work at that time, and saw nothing of all this; nor would D. B. have aroused my attention if he had known, for he felt that there were ruins enough nearer the sea to keep me happy, and now and then would remark, in a reluctant way, that ruins were not intended for consular tours. This was a poor argument, quickly demolished, for what can be more useful in a country of scattered official groups, like Turkey, than to see the British Consul in places where he has never been seen before—even if it means delightful days spent in crossing places where he is not seen at all? Such was the Doric peninsula for most of its empty length. One boat drawn up by a solitary hut, and one far-scattered village; and here and there olive terraces that came down to small estuaries, flat triangles fringed with willows or even palms, dry except in flood-time. But most of the hours were spent in and out of the sun and shadow of high cliffs, where the sea-ducks were surprised at their swimming, and the clear green water in its depths was so beguiling that it made the rocks look like malachite below. Under a deep overhang we anchored, bathed and slept through the hot hours: and woke up to find that one of our hens had laid an egg into the sea.

Mehmet was responsible for these animals. It must be admitted that one can easily starve on the coasts of Caria, so he bought six of them in a cage at Budrum, lashed it to the side of the prow with a pan of maize beside it, and fed us on chicken when the country provided no supplies. D. B., who did the housekeeping, and had been brought face to face with reality by a meal or two of potatoes, had authorized the hens —though he averted his eyes from the desecration of his deck. But Mehmet loved untidiness for its own sake and was delighted with them; his long Kurdish face and narrow eyes and philosopher's bush of white hair bent brooding above them: he made hen-like noises; and they fluffed out their feathers, brave but ladylike, answered with refined and peevish cluckings, and craned their necks at every wave that rode below their cage. Punctual under difficulties, they laid their unexpected egg; and we saw it, deep in the greenness of the sea, unattainable for all D. B.'s diving.

The Doric peninsula widens out to the group of villages and little anchorage of Datcha, where a road, with a daily bus that takes twelve hours, comes down from Marmaris, and a steamer stops once a fortnight if asked to do so. Here there was a *Kaymakam*, a hotel and a new school building, and a feeling of prosperity and security very different from the days of Newton, when pirates hung around and money was smuggled 'as if contraband', and people could only negotiate a bill if a mail steamer called. Yet even now it is a local and a small prosperity, not the old sea-going traffic of the ancient capital—whose walls show at the foot of the sea-hills nearby.[1] A few scattered rowing-boats, like worn-out shoes, lay on the edge of the sands; the life was inland, and the *Kaymakam* offered to take us to see it in Kara Köy, a village where the road ends and the westward track begins. A feast, said he, happened that day to be celebrating the circumcision of twelve little boys.

There was an immediate easiness in the landscape when we left the sea. Carob, oleander and almond, the myrtle whose boughs are tied to the tombstones, and Vallonia oak trees with frilly acorns like ruffs—exported for tanning—filled the shallow valleys; the sharp slopes behind were dark with pines. No panthers are here, they say, but bears and wild boars. An ancient temenos stood by the road that leads to Reshidiye, the main centre of the district, a townlet of thirteen hundred souls. Kara Köy lay to the west, on higher ground. Its up-and-down houses and roofs were crowded with people, and lorry-loads were arriving all the time. Groups of women stood with clean white kerchiefs held over heads and mouths; the young men walked about behind a drum, trumpet and violin; the twelve little boys, the heroes of the day but disregarded, wandered with mixed feelings, and wore embroidered handkerchiefs and tassels stuffed with holy earth to distinguish them from the crowd. Only one of them was rich, spangled with gold coins, but not much happier for that: their moment had not yet come, and we were all intent on feasting.

D. B. sat with the Elders, and I found a circle in a harim where the food came in a more easy-going way but hotter— flaps of unleavened bread, soup, makarna (macaroni), stew, rissoles, beans, yaourt, and rice, and a sweet sticky paste: we dipped it all up from bowls set on the floor. The houses were as clean as the Swiss; their wooden cupboards and stairs were bare and scrubbed; and the people left their shoes as they came in and wiped their feet on a towel at the stair's foot. They were rough folk and mostly plain to look at, with the excellent manners of the Turkish village, the result of a sure and sound tradition handed from generation to generation, which breaks into gaiety when ceremony demands it, as an earth-feeding stream breaks into the sun.

There was a bustle now, the doctor had arrived; his razors wrapped in newspapers were laid on a packing-case; the men all crowded into the largest room as audience. A seat in the front row was placed for D. B. and another for me; the other women remained in their own room, a mother or grandmother stepping out to look round the corner when it was the turn of her child. The rich son of the house, eleven years old, was now seated in the face of all on a chair, frightened but brave; his infantile penis clipped in a sort of pliers; a wipe of disinfectant to the razor, and the moment was over: the child, with a startled look, as if the knowledge that virility has its pains were first breaking upon him, wrung his mouth in his hand to cover his cry, while the men in the room clapped, and someone outside fired a pistol; when the ceremonies were over the child was seated on a bed; visitors as they passed dropped small coins into a handkerchief laid out beside him; and the little creature was out of the harim—a man.

About four in the afternoon we were with *Elfin* again in the solitudes of the sea—no boat in sight, no habitation, but widespaced, crowded shoals of capes and islands. They ringed and enclosed the horizon, and the sunset swam here and there among them like a goldfish in a bowl. A pharos began to shine on Syme, and a forest fire seemed to be burning farther away on Rhodes. We had still not made our anchorage. Hüseyin found it in the dark, padded in a softness of trees under the ageing moon. Next morning, without seeing a human being, again we made eastward, and found Balikashiran, the Fishes' Leap, a narrow fjord between pine-clothed slopes, which ends at the isthmus where, according to Herodotus, the lands of Cnidus ended.

Here, he says, when Harpagus and the Persians were coming, the Cnidians began to dig a trench to keep them out; but they got tired of the splinters of the stone that cut their eyes, and sent to Delphi to ask what was the matter: and the Pythoness answered that if Zeus had wanted an island he would have made one himself. So they gave themselves up to the Persians.

The isthmus is declared to be a kilometre wide, though both D. B. and I thought it wider. Spratt in 1838 and Myres in 1893 found traces of the ancient cutting, and the Symiots, before 1912, were in the habit of hauling small boats across it. D. B. and I, hunting for the place, climbed through a little patch of roses that had gone back to wildness, by a woodcutter's path that led us to the ridge, and there the northern coast appeared with curving beaches and green capes, and the mainland rose in slopes of heath and cistus, broom, rosemary and myrtle, to

pointed pine-covered ranges, and to the smooth limestone
plateau behind Halicarnassus out of sight. Surprisingly, in
the houseless loneliness, the motor road ran at our feet, bringing its daily bus to the six thousand inhabitants that now live
in the lands of Cnidus; and it is only in sight of these long
empty distances that one can properly admire the effort the
Turkish government are making to bring communications to
their scattered people along the distant bays. Their last
election was won by roads, schools and water conduits supplied
to the peasants, who now realize that votes secure these things;
and no future government will be wise to neglect them. The
revolution has been quietly effected, giving the men on the land,
the Turkish majority, a knowledge of their power in the state.

In the vast and empty view, four soldiers were sitting by
the roadside, mending the telegraph wire that ran across
country on any handy tree-trunk in its way. We passed by,
and soon found the narrowest point, where boats could be
drawn across the isthmus over boggy land bright with a small-
leaved maple found nowhere else in the world; they call it
günlük agach and it is government property, and its trunks
contain a medicinal glue which they export to Germany.
Under its gay leaves a few thin cows were grazing, with a
cowherd's hut, and his bee-hives, nearby, built of hollow pine-
trunks piled together in the sun; they have come down unaltered from the days when Carian honey was exported
overseas.

Herodotus speaks rather slightingly of the Carian behaviour;
they were brought into bondage by Harpagus, he says, without
having done any glorious deeds, either they or the Greeks that
dwell in their country. This was at the beginning of the great
age of Greece, whose many variations seem more like a mountain range, with higher and lower peaks and valleys, than like
a single summit which humanity climbs up and down. One
wonders what makes the watershed, and where an age of

The Doric Peninsula

decadence begins, while actual human beings continue to appear identical at birth.

After birth, climate, food, and many material things come into play. But these do not explain a same people in a same place, strong in itself at one time and weak at another. Circumstances alone are not enough. 'There must be some cause, some good reason, why the Greeks were so eager for liberty then, and now are eager for servitude. There was something, men of Athens, something in the hearts of the multitude then, which there is not now.' This, in 341 B.C., was Demosthenes' passionate question, and we continue to ask it always. For there must be an alteration, to make human creatures different who begin by being the same; and if it is not, as we say, inborn, the difference must lie in the *direction* in which a man is taught to go.

In the 4th century B.C. the sculpture of the Greek world changed. It acquired movement. Man, no longer firmly planted, was shown with grace and drama shifting his weight from one foot to the other in the act of motion. It is the process of transition which, if uncertain or undirected, becomes a decline: and the human movement is the same. If, as it passes from one step to the next one, the hope, the joy, are lost—the fault is not in the being whose possibilities remain unaltered, but in the goal to which his face is set. The free choice of one age fails in the next, either because its transition is uncertain, or because, out of fear, it does not stir at all; then it stiffens into an obstacle; and the river of time foams over it and destroys it.

Classical greatness is *passion*, whether of thought or action— the wholeness of a community, as of an individual, flowing in one direction, without negation or reservation, and in co-incidence with Time. This coincidence and this unity give that illusion of stillness which we call serenity; and while the unity with Time remains unbroken, the heroic age continues.

82

The task of a statesman

The whole business of the statesman and the teacher is to keep these two separate processions, of the human being and of Time, together. And Time, which is rather a vague expression, I take in this connection to mean all those circumstances which are going on around but are not intrinsically a part of the orbit of a man's life, and with it make up the climate of his age.

The statesman, like the caricaturist, must choose few strokes for his picture and only the ones that matter. It is a difficult, but a simple, task. Direction and pace are his instruments, to keep his age in step with Time, and therefore great; or to speed it up or slow it down, so as to rectify some out-of-step condition of the past and so produce an age of change; or to let it move out of step with its own day—either faster or slower—when the consequence that we call decadence will follow, and the children of his own and many later generations will have to struggle in the cross-currents of decay. Things good in themselves—the tradition of a village or the faith of a Demosthenes—perfectly valid in the integrity of their origins, become fetters if they cannot alter. Not permanence but change, its pace and its direction, are all that matter. The human creature must shift his weight from one step to the next one; and to make him do it without either hesitation or haste is the statesman's task.

No human good that we know is outside our temporal orbit. Few—very few—of our attainments are so profound that they are valid for always; even if they are so, they need adjustment, a straightening here, a loosening there, like an old garment to be fitted to the body! and men will submit to this, if they can believe in the rightness of the aim; for who would not make for his own welfare if he were *sure*? So Socrates thought, assuming that the good need only be recognized to be pursued: and the uncertainty of the recognition in his day —the demand for the search so to say—was the symptom of a discord in time, produced by unyielding and unadapted loyalties—patriotism and religion most of all.

Patriotism in particular has ever been thought of as a sign of the worthiness of nations, preserving them from being taught in ways contrary to their own needs. It saves them from alien impositions which may put them out of tune with their reality and produce that vacillation which is the decadence of nations. It limits them to home-made mistakes. Yet a conqueror can be beneficial, if his aim and his age agree. History has to roll by to make the process visible, and the Greeks of the 4th century B.C. scarcely saw by what steps they were advancing into the larger unity of Alexander's world. It was not decline but transition—but so confused and hesitating, so clogged by shibboleths and clichés, that the name of decadence has often been applied.

In the generations after Alexander, when the Athenian Empire was over and had indeed become sterile to itself, the cities of Asia still had a long and vivid run before them. They had stumbled when they tied themselves to Greece. It was one of those mistakes on which 'decadence' often follows, and indeed the free Ionian glory never returned. And though one cannot regret anything that built Athens in the prospect of the ages, yet there are two points of view over every omelet; the point of view of the cities of Asia is that of the eggs.

It is not irrelevant to think of such things today, for the riddle and the task are perpetual. When I was a small girl listening at table to the talk of my elders, Mr. Ramsay MacDonald took the side of the Boers in South Africa, and foreshadowed a theory which has since been evolved and partly carried out —opposite as can be to the ancient practice—that an imperial power keeps, as far as it can, no nation tied against its will. On top of this innovation, the later theory of Alexander's united world is making its way, with a natural strain developing between the two. In modern dilemmas like those of Cyprus, the history of the 4th century B.C. and the Athenian, British and Macedonian methods might well be studied and compared. The problems, the troubles, the thoughts of later Greek history are very much our own.

It is a pity perhaps that we chiefly study a classical age which we do not look like imitating, rather than the Hellenistic and the Greco-Roman, full of examples and warnings: for they were working through wars, through revolutions, federations and monarchies, towards unity. However imperfectly attained and uncertain in its harmony, this was their step in history. Innumerable particularisms comparable to modern nationalisms impeded; the great powers, with Helots in Laconia, with cleruchies on the islands, threw dark shadows; the continuation of small autonomies retarded the whole process. These hindrances made the Greek world uncertain and out of tune: they brought to an end a great age which could only have continued if a perception of unity had prevailed and transformed it.

The notion flashed by with Alexander like a wing in the sun. It showed, as it passed, how the capacity for greatness persists; and as it faded in darkness, it left behind it in the barbarian night—like a touchstone, or Cinderella slipper on the steps of the Greek palace—the civilization by which we live today.

9

LORYMA

The Persian Gold

It is not in Attica that the war will be decided ... but in the countries by which Attica is supported.

THUCYDIDES III, 13.

All the generals who have ever sailed from Athens ... take money from the Chians, from Erythraeans ... I mean from the people who dwell in Asia.
DEMOSTHENES, On the Chersonese, 24.

THE MORNING WAS ALREADY FALLING TO PIECES ABOUT US, when *Elfin* made her way south-west from the isthmus of Cnidus, across the openings of wooded empty bays. We were back on the limestone coast, distinct from the rusty tumult of Caria, and the shores had grown even more solemn, as if cathedral aisles were standing in the sea. One could imagine no base to them, so steep and high and into such a darkness of water did they go. The limestone was white where the waves had washed it, smoothed by their kneading but furrowed with deep meanders, as if giant sponges had turned to stone along the water-line. There were black streaks of old rains beating; otherwise, slanting in shadow, the cliffs were grey like the doves that inhabit them, with a biscuit colour of sunlight above. They were scattered with pale mauve candytuft and other sorts of limestone autumn flowers.

Elfin, moving delicately and slowly—because D. B. was fishing—added to this feeling of awe, like a respectful sightseer wandering quietly under the majestic traceries. Nor were we alone. At the border of the rock the water eats a hollow, so that the sea edge lies as if on a thin black line of emptiness.

Conon

Here the sun can only strike upwards through depth, as if indeed the cathedral walls were descending into darkness and the brilliance of their windows were shining from below; and in this shadow, not more than a stone's throw away, a seal was fishing also. Its sleek head moved and dived with a demure, preoccupied air, like a young woman walking down a street when she is aware but has no wish to be followed. She paid us no attention, but slipped along her cool track with the Aegean's siren voices, a subtle liquid melody of water and rocks, about her.

We were now approaching that narrowest point between the mainland and Rhodes, where the Loryma promontory pushes out its rocky hands. The whole length of the Doric peninsula lies opposite in the north, festooned by outer islands that look like an enclosure.

Eleven years after Aegospotami and his flight with the eight ships, Conon with Pharnabazus, heading from Rhodes in 394 B.C., here fought the fleet of the Spartan Peisander.

A long odyssey, from Hellespont to Cyprus and into the Persian service, brought the Athenian sailor to his revenge. As admiral of the enemy's navy, the Spartans blockaded him in Caunus; the nearest Persian governors, hurrying to relieve him, chased them back to Rhodes with all their fleet. Conon had left little to chance during his exile. He had travelled inland through Cilicia, across Euphrates, and persuaded the Persian King in Babylon to appoint a paymaster to supply funds in abundance as he might assign them, so that his soldiers, deprived for fifteen months of pay, were not disbanded. He had also asked for any Persian he might choose as a commander and, with singular wisdom, selected Pharnabazus, and so ensured success. In 395, he persuaded the Rhodians to revolt, and was received with all his ships in their harbour; and an Egyptian fleet, carrying five hundred thousand measures of grain for the Spartans, was captured as it approached what it thought a friendly port. To Rhodes, so stored with grain, Persian ships from the south sailed in—ten from Cilicia and eighty under the lord of the Sidonians. A Syracusan had seen their preparations in Phoenicia a year before and carried the news to Greece.

Now, in 394, the Persian fleet was based on Loryma with more than ninety triremes. Peisander, the Spartan, brother-in-law of King Agesilaus, set out from Cnidus with only eighty-five. There was a skirmish, and then—in sight as it were of *Elfin* across the Doric bay—the fleet of Pharnabazus and the Sidonians, with Conon and his Greek ships in the van, moved northward in close formation, and met Peisander's line of battle not far from the Cnidian shore.

Peisander was brave but not a sailor, and, since Sparta was unpopular, the Asiatic Greeks, his allies on the left wing, immediately fled; he himself was driven ashore, his trireme damaged by the enemy's beaks. All the others, also driven ashore, abandoned their ships and made their escape as best they could to Cnidus, but he fell fighting: the Spartan sea supremacy was over. Conon and Pharnabazus induced Cos and Nisyros, Teos, Chios, Mitylene, Ephesus and Erythrae to secede—'the same eagerness infected all the cities', for the Persian promised to leave them independent and to set up no fortifications within their walls. The people received this announcement with joy, and sent gifts of friendship to Pharnabazus; for Conon had advised him that, if he acted in this way, the cities would be friendly, but would give trouble if he should appear to wish to enslave them.

Pharnabazus spent the winter restoring his lands of the north that the Spartans had harried. At the opening of the spring, with ships and mercenaries, he and Conon sailed through the islands, to the mainland of Greece; and Conon then asked for the fleet, promising to maintain it by contributions from the islands, so that he might put in to help Athens to rebuild her walls: Pharnabazus 'eagerly despatched him . . . and gave him additional money for the rebuilding.'[1]

These were the walls that eleven years before had been demolished, under the Spartans' eyes in the starving city, to the sound of the playing of flute girls, at the end of the Peloponnesian war—the walls that Themistocles had inspired. On his arrival, Conon erected a large part of them, giving his own crews for the work, paying the wages of carpenters and masons, and meeting whatever other expense was necessary; and it is not hard to imagine what must have been alive in his heart.

But the Spartans saw Athens raising her head, and sent to Tiribazus, the new Satrap in Lydia, to plead that they made no claim to Greek cities in Asia, but wished for all (in Europe) to be independent; and though the Persian King was reluctant to abandon the Athenians, the Peace of Antalcidas, or the King's Peace, was the end of it all, six years after the rebuilding of the walls. Conon disappears, put to death by Tiribazus or dying in Cyprus of illness. An inscription in Athens declared that 'he set free the allies of the Athenians', the cities of Asia, and for that brief interval, while he and Pharnabazus worked together, the words of the inscription were true.[2]

Autonomy, the cities' dream, we have seen in the last two chapters was not irreconcilable with the (financial) requirements of Persia, nor with double engagements, in one form or another, with Persia and Athens too. But it was incompatible with an Athenian Empire in the west that, whenever it became effective, roused the hostility of Persia, and, when it was ineffective, could offer no protection. The sea security was largely provided by the money and put into effect by the ships of the cities and islands themselves; they could attend to it and to their commerce too, as Rhodes was to demonstrate later; and when the Persians were kept from the coastline during the first few decades after Salamis, the trading cities probably found this separation not so happy a circumstance after all. As time went on, it became plain to anyone who looked into it that the pressure of a western profiteer near at hand was heavier than that of an eastern one at a distance.

When the Peloponnesian war came to the east, the misery increased. Sentiment, which had tilted the balance—the profound attachment of the Greek to his origins—began to lose its power. It must never be underrated: when the Greeks of Asia found someone from the mainland who cared about them —the Spartan Agesilaus for instance—their attachment was impulsive and devoted; when he left they wept and followed him, to fight for him in Greece. Sentiment led them, as it led Conon to rebuild the walls of Athens, ruining the goodwill of Persia because of the remembrance of the empire in his heart; as it led Demosthenes to wear himself away against the new unity of Philip. These were among those brave men 'who repose in the public monuments, all of whom alike, as being worthy of the same honour, the country buries . . . not only the successful or victorious';[3] though they may not have seen clearly, the world is the richer for their lives. But if they are to serve us, we are bound to search where and how their ways misled them, and not to call a mistake by other names: and in the dealings between Greece and her colonies, must admit that neither Athens nor Sparta, in the days of their power, ever dealt kindly for any length of time with the cities of Asia, whose safety and independence could only have been maintained on a neutral ridge between the east and west.

A few references sufficiently illustrate the callousness of Greece towards the Asiatic Greeks. The treaties of 412 B.C. between Sparta and Tissaphernes, argued over by Lichas and the other commissioners in Cnidus, agree that 'the cities the King has, or the King's ancestors had, shall be the King's'. When the quarrel with Tissaphernes was made up the same year, and a new treaty signed in the Maeander plain, the words were scarcely altered. 'The country in Asia shall be the King's, and the King shall treat his own country as he pleases.' The Spartan commissioners cared nothing for Asia; what they disliked was the authority of Persia in *Greece,* which had been implicit in the former treaties.[4]

The next references come in the same year from the Athenians in Samos, who were ready to cede without opposition the whole of Ionia and the adjacent islands, and comforted themselves for being divorced from their home government by the thought that their fleet could compel the cities of the empire to give them money, just as if they still were based on Athens.[5]

Another example is the notorious peace of the Spartan envoy Antalcidas, 'the King's Peace', as it was known at the time. It provided, in 386 B.C., that the cities in Asia should belong to the King, as well as Clazomenae and Cyprus among the islands, and that the other cities should be left independent;[6] and although this treaty was odious in its day, it so closely resembles all that preceded it as far as Asia is concerned, that one is again inclined to attribute its unpopularity to the increase of Persian power in *Greece*, rather than to any sudden chivalry towards the Asiatic mainland towns. The only noticeable improvement is that it implies the liberty of the islands.

With such a pattern of empire, of a nature to deprave all who have to do with it,[7] one can hardly be surprised that, after the Sicilian catastrophe, none showed more alacrity than the subjects of the Athenians who were everywhere willing even beyond their power to revolt.[8]   They swung from Athens to Sparta, and then, when Lysander planted his thugs among them, swung back to Athens, and away again, in a sad pendulum. 'Some of our states pressed by war would sooner open their gates to a besieger than to a relief force from Athens.'[9]

This was said by Isocrates in the middle of the 4th century. By that time a crusade against Persia was in the air, and the liberation of the Asiatic cities became a useful catchword; but at the back of it, the feeling was still for Greece and not for

Asia—despair of any other unity, a fear of the homeless army of war-stranded men, and the growing difficulty of the mercenary armies. 'Undertake to establish soldiers in this region' (from Cilicia to the Black Sea), says Isocrates to Philip, 'and to settle those who now, for lack of the daily necessities of life are wandering from place to place committing outrages. If you do not stop these men from banding together, by providing sufficient livelihood for them, they will grow . . . into so great a multitude as to be a terror no less to the Hellenes than to the barbarians. Consider . . . what a disgrace it is to sit idly by and see Asia flourishing more than Europe.'[10]

The Athenian sympathy is graded by the riches of Asia; for Athens needed a steady flow of wealth. She could perhaps have obtained it without empire—with a strong navy and the alliance of the cities at the cross-roads of traffic; the profit of the eastern trade could have paid for Parthenon and Propylaea as it had once paid for the splendour of Miletus, with enough left over for the Persian revenue as well. But moderation, a rarer virtue than charity, was required. As for Sparta, she had little but a nuisance interest in Asia at all times, and without Persian help would have had no chance across the sea.

Money made the history. Either Persia or the Asiatic cities direct had to produce it. 'We have no money,' says Alcibiades: 'but the enemy have an abundance from the King.' And he and his colleagues went raiding—collecting in Macedonia, Thasos, Cyzicus and Selymbria and the tithes of the shipping of Pontus; in the Hellespont and Chalcedon, and large sums from Halicarnassus and all down the western coast—by means of which he lost the battle of Notium, but gained Byzantium, whence the Spartan commander was absent on a financial expedition also, asking Pharnabazus for money.

Money was the chronic difficulty.

'What greater gladness can there be than to have to flatter no one in the world, Greek or barbarian, for the sake of pay?'

Money

One sympathizes with the Spartan admiral's heartfelt words; and then one sympathizes with the boats he captured sailing in with fish and vegetables from the islands, and sold to give the soldiers a month's wages; or with the Chians whom he called together and forced to contribute, so that the sailors might not threaten them. It was to avoid this sort of extortion that the people of Asia paid what Demosthenes calls benevolences, and the Chians gave—to another of the Spartan admirals —five pieces of money for each man.

The ultimate financial weapon remained with Persia until Alexander's day—secretly at first, and then more and more openly, until it came to be constantly apparent and generally recognized. By the winter of 412 B.C., Tissaphernes was distributing wages to the Spartan ships at the rate of an Attic drachma (about 4/–) a day for each man (soon to be reduced). It was always the King and his money. As the 4th century advanced, the position grew more and more notorious. In 395 B.C., Timocrates of Rhodes was sent to Greece by the King, to bribe up a war against the Spartans and deflect their troops from Asia. Agesilaus—ordered home to attend to it —remarked that ten thousand archers (the emblem on the King's coin) were responsible for his recall.[11]

The Great King became the arbiter in Greece. 'How many embassies did we not despatch,' says Isocrates, 'to convince him that it was neither just nor expedient for one state to dominate the Hellenes.' And thirty years or little more before the march of Alexander, 'was it not he' (the Persian King), Isocrates cries again, 'who decided the issue of the war . . . who directed the terms of the peace; and is it not he who presides over our affairs? Do we not sail off to him as to a master? Do we not in our wars against each other, cast our hopes of salvation on him?'[12]

Even Demosthenes repeats the old cry: 'The Satraps of Asia . . . will urge the Persian King to supply us with money;

and . . . he has such influence over proceedings here, that in our former wars with Lacedaemon, whichever side he joined he caused them to vanquish their opponents, and now siding with us he will easily beat down the power of Philip.'[13]

The Cnidians were no different from the rest, when they thought the rock splinters in their eyes more unpleasant than the Persians at a distance!

As we neared the prongs of the Loryma headland, a bright sea came beating up the Rhodian channel, whipped by the *embat*—the afternoon wind that blows upon the land. We were running westward between two mountain ranges, of which one showed and one was only a row of stony heaps that proved its existence under water. When we got out of their shelter, the north-west wind, said D. B., would sweep down on *Elfin*; so we put her into a cove, restless but safe, while we lunched and considered; and this was one of the many delights of our voyage—that at any moment we could make a new decision, stop or go, turn left or right, cross a bay's mouth or coast in its recesses. Like the cities of Asia, we were enjoying our freedom though things stronger than ourselves were in control. The problem was whether the wind would let *Elfin* get round the corner to Loryma.

When we sailed here again, two years later, D. B. had followed the route quite often; he spoke of it in a familiar way as 'the usual round'. But this, in 1952, was *Elfin*'s first adventure so far into the south. Nor had we descriptions of the mainland to guide us: neither Newton nor Leake nor Fellows, nor anyone I knew except Mr. G. E. Bean who has walked everywhere, had travelled here: the headlands and the inlets we were now approaching, the Peraea of the Rhodians, are among the least visited and loneliest, the most pathless, gaunt, and rocky of all the promontories of the Turkish shores.

We had passed by a few uprooted vineyards, a church and a village recently crumbled, and some rare living traces of

94

tended trees and terraces of corn: but the people and their villages were hidden in the centre of the promontory, built hollow as a bowl to hold them. The shelter we could find there was not very good, for it faced to the north; and Hüseyin, looking out at the rather unsteady horizon, thought that the wind would drop and we might make Loryma by sunset. It is perhaps the trickiness of these waters that causes fishing-boats to be so scarce; we had only seen one since leaving the harbour of Cnidus, with three Carians inside it under a ragged ochre sail—its gunwale aslant and dipping against dark waves.

As the sun was about to set we reached and turned the head-land rocks in a froth of foam, saw an unbroken fortress wall as the 3rd-century Rhodians or Ptolemies had built it, and steered through a gap below it into an almost land-locked pool. The last light caught the three square southern and the great round western tower—built of rectangular blocks, convex and perfectly fitted without mortar. There was just—only just—time for a photograph. From a two-roomed guardhouse, the only building except the fort in sight, three soldiers were watching; the sun was going; I could clamber up rocks and scrub if I jumped ashore; and D. B.—the most active, under-standing person in an emergency one could wish for—handed me out and began to anchor while I struggled with the slope. It was only when I had secured my pictures that I looked back and saw a fracas going on: the three soldiers had arrived, with three rifles on their shoulders, and were listening with an un-sympathetic look while D. B. explained in unmistakable but not very grammatical Turkish what and who a consul is. To deal with landscape as if it belongs to one has gone out in our day. It was always stimulating to see D. B. revive the old-fashioned assumption that the red ensign and *Elfin*, demure and inoffensive as they might appear, had a right to be on any bit of sea or land they happened to occupy at the moment.

The soldiers disagreed. They repeated, as they came fol-

lowing us over the rocks, that one does not land before report-
ing to the guardhouse; they looked at the sun and my camera,
which I pointed at to explain my hurry, as if they could see no
connection between them; they walked, one behind each of
us, with increasing glumness as we made the circuit of the
oblong *enceinte* and its towers.   While D. B. continued to pour
reproof on the sergeant in front, I tried more feminine methods
with my soldiers in the rear—never, I may say, with less
success.   Not for a moment did their expression relax.   The
wall, which looked five feet or so in width, and its great
blocks, from which the upper tiers had fallen, still made a
chemin de ronde for us to walk on.   I asked them to help me
up and down quite easy places, and this they did with looks of
unflattering reluctance: I thought it was good for them to
have their minds distracted from their rifles, and helping
people up and down walls makes it difficult to think of shooting
too; between one thought and another, a neutralizing process
is set up in the mind.   But there was anyway no danger.
D. B.'s method, unjust as it was, was successful; the undesira-
bility, the tactlessness, the criminality of bothering consuls grew
with every step along the wall: my heart went out to the little
garrison, whose only visit this probably was, and all its cordiality
spoilt.

"Do give them a cigarette," I said to D. B., when we had
reached *Elfin* again and they were setting off in the dinghy with
Hüseyin and all the papers.

"Cigarette?" said he, still seething with the outrage.   "As
soon as I get back, I shall report them."   The little party went
without a smile.

In the stillness of Loryma we spent the night.

The wind could be heard howling outside, against the
hills that enclosed our sheltered water as if it were a mountain
tarn.   Only a fanning ripple touched the centre.   The sound
of the wind, inarticulate and busy like the world's voice, gave

an illusion of safety, of an unassailable peace. If it could penetrate, how many sleeping echoes would it waken? Athenians from Samos, dodging the Dorian Cnidus, picking up ships' tackle at Syme, sheltering at Loryma; Conon, before the battle, with his ninety ships; the Roman fleet that dared not face Hannibal in the offing;[14] Cassius, gathering forces against Rhodes, twenty miles away.[15] Each in their turn passed through the narrow opening and felt the sudden calm. In these places, the natural features have remained unaltered; the moments that visit them, fashioned to one pattern by nature itself, drop like beads on a string, through long pauses, one after the other, into the same silence.

10

THE RHODIAN PERAEA

Civilization and the Middle Class

Sea-girt Rhodes, child of Aphrodite and bride of Helios . . . nigh to a promontory of spacious Asia.

PINDAR, 7th, Olympian.

And while committing to hope the uncertainty of final success, in the business before them they thought fit to act boldly and trust in themselves.

Pericles' speech, THUCYDIDES II. 42.

W E HAD NOW TURNED THE CORNER OF THE RHODIAN sea. We were nearing southern shores which the Greeks, in the days before Alexander, visited more rarely than Ionia. Carian and Lycian had been spoken here, even on the coast; and inland, at Cibyra, Lycian remained in use in Strabo's day. A remoteness more ancient perhaps and certainly more primitive than we had met before lay over these promontories, under pine trees that dipped their boughs out of unknown forests from clearer glades into deeper waters, as if *Elfin* had turned into a region where anything might happen, in bewitched Aegean Broceliandes.

As she turned east out of the whipping wind and sun of the Rhodian channel under the immense sheer ramparts and pathless bulwarks of the southern face of the Peraea, one wondered how there ever could have been a connection between Rhodes the civilized commercial city, its open harbours, its closed arsenals, its riches, conversation, and learning, and this unyielding sovereignty of rock. An older Rhodes might perhaps be imagined—where Saturn's scythe was made and Helen came when Menelaus was dead. There the native queen's handmaidens, dressed up as Furies, hung her on a tree, and the sanctuary remained.[1] One could think of it under the lee of the high fortresses—Phoenix, and another one in sight whose name we did not know. Their inaccessible walls, coloured and darkly shining as if they were prows of the hills they stood on, could just be distinguished from the tiny deck of *Elfin*. We seemed to be standing inside one of those pictures where a knight, a small figure on a horse, blows his horn at a landscape surmounted by towers. The towers did not show: only, through glasses, the smooth-cut face of the walls, functional as anything made in the age of metal, and with the same stripped beauty. But we had no thought of scaling, nor were we challenging: there must be inland ways, and no one would climb from the east. This was the outpost where the great Rhodian republic, garrisoned with Cretan mercenaries, kept the channel of her shipping free. Here she overlooked the passage from Egypt and Syria, and swept away the Aegean pirates, and first among sea-powers kept a naval law; until the envy of Rome destroyed her.

"I will leave you the sun," said Cassius.

The Rhodian Peraea

Her three thousand statues have vanished, and her streets that appeared decorated from every angle, where no small house stood beside a big one, but all were uniform; and the walls that were beacons for Greek sailors. They have been replaced by later fortifications, and the horses of the sun stand in exile, in Venice over the doors of St. Mark.

Like Miletus, and for a long time more fortunate in her sieges, Rhodes carried her civilization through from the Minoan age: the legend goes that Apollo first claimed the island 'waxing from its roots in earth beneath the hoary sea.'[2] The slim bodies of animals with slanting eyes round her vases come from a long distance; and the first inhabitants, the Telchines, who were reputed maligners and sorcerers, who poured the water of Styx mixed with sulphur on animals and plants to destroy them, were in fact, according to Strabo, excellent workmen from Crete and Cyprus.

This international character at the cross-roads was held by the city through the later centuries of her greatness. Like Cos, her three early towns coalesced, and Hippodamus of Miletus, who built Piraeus and Priene, was said to have founded the new Rhodes in the shape of a theatre, with three ports open to all the markets of the Aegean.

Newton found a town too large for its inhabitants and an unsafe anchorage in winter where Strabo had been unable to speak of any other city as equal or even as almost equal to Rhodes. Here Caesar studied, and Pompey came to visit, and Cicero stopped as a retiring governor on his way.[3] During the great siege, in 304 B.C., Protogenes continued to paint in his garden in the suburbs, while the King's sentinels watched over him and Demetrius preferred to lose the chance of a victory rather than his picture.[4]

This story has a fabricated air, but the arts, at all events, were loved in Rhodes. Even a monument built during captivity, which showed the conquering Artemisia of Caria triumphant over the prostrate city, was preserved as sacred, though hidden as a humiliating remembrance behind a wall;[5] and the Colossus lay on the ground, broken by earthquake—its pieces, after nearly a thousand years, to be carted on nine hundred camels from Loryma, sold by the Arabs to a Hama Jew.[6]

It was cast in the early 3rd century B.C., when Rhodes was reaching the height of her greatness. Her full citizenship soon extended to the mainland coast, from Cnidus to Physcus, which is now Marmaris. Her silver became the standard for Asia Minor and the islands. She kept the freedom of the seas and governed her people with care, inheriting the Athenian banking and the traffic in corn, and opening African markets as far as Numidia. As well as she could, she avoided the embroilments that followed the death of Alexander, and reacted only when her commerce was threatened. "I am master of the world," said Antoninus, "but it is the Rhodian law that rules it."

As we sailed under the high rocks of the Peraea, the glory of Rhodes, so unanimously praised by the ancient world, seemed to fill the western horizon like a tide. It rose beyond the limits of sight in the dawn of history, and gathered its momentum and glittered, poised in a few centuries' perfection, under the Aegean sun; and through another long period subsided—with waves here and there of Roman, Byzantine, Arab, and Christian—whose last fortified walls are still there. The Germans defended them, from the Grand Master's palace to the gate of St. George; the people of Auvergne, from St. George to the Spanish tower; the English along the wall to St. Mary—of which the upper storey was held by Aragonese and the rest by Provence, and by the Italians who reached St. Catharine's gate that leads to the harbour. The sea-wall was held by Portugal and Castile, and the French went on to the Grand Master's palace, along the northern side.

In 1522 the last siege ended, and Suleiman the Magnificent

took the city. Most of the inhabitants made their escape, some to Italy, others to Candia, leaving the island almost uninhabited; until Randolph, one hundred and sixty years later, found 'many Greeks returned, and it is now very well peopled. The Basha hath the revenues of the island and some other small islands adjacent, towards the maintaining five galleys. . . . He hath a great love for his slaves, not suffering any to abuse them. To the north of the town he hath built a large bagno, very commodious for them, where is a very neat chapel with two altars, one for the Roman priests, the other for the Greek. . . . The walls are in very bad repair'.[7] In the 19th century Newton saw the brass guns of the Knights, with vents protected from the weather by the cuirasses from their armoury; and found the tomb of Fabrizio del Carretto, the last Grand Master to be buried on his island, in the church of St. John.

The Italians came, and rebuilt with piety medieval walls and quays on ancient foundations; and now the Greeks are back, living their lively days as if in a shrunken hollow of their sea. The trees of their island and the tops of its towers show a broken outline, as if they too were waves tossing to settle in the ebbing afternoon: and as I watched them, the problem of the century round which this book is written tormented me: the slow rise from darkness, the brief perfection, the long decline.

> The lyf so short, the craft so long to lerne,
> Th'assay so sharp, so harsh the conquerynge,
> The dredful joye, alwey that slit so yerne,
> Al this mene I be love . . .[8]

Not only love—each life flows to its moment, of which the greatest art can only be the memory—a gilding that recalls the vanished gold. In their history too the nations reach their climax and lose it; they graze it and drift away, like swimmers in hard waters. Is it stability that they touch in the brief perfection, or does that perfection float rootless, to be met but never to be kept? This must be the chief of all things for students of history to study, and indeed for anyone else who wishes to discover the world as it is.

The great ages pass swiftly—the 5th century in Attica, the 15th in Italy, the 18th in England. Their ruins last after them longer than they do, with an immobility perhaps equivalent to man's fondness for static laws. But the great age while it lives, when civilization touches its height, moves freely, using its past as if it were alive and not a boundary wall as it becomes in its decline. And there is usually a similarity between such periods—produced by the prosperous middle class that makes them—the bankers, merchants, country gentry, builders and captains of ships. Other more imperial ages may be richer; they may exploit or enjoy what has been nurtured before them; they may spread farther, and—nearly always—last longer: but the secret of life is not in them; the fire they kindle is not their own fire; the settled magnificence of Rome is different in kind from the nature of Greece as she rises, or Florence as she remembers, or England as she builds.

Generalizations, one is told, are dangerous. So is life, for that matter, and it is built up on generalization—from the earliest effort of the adventurer who dared to eat a second berry because the first had not killed him. So I will stick to my generalizing, and hold that the summit of civilization is touched by the middle class. It walks along a razor's edge between the tyrant and the proletariat and is short-lived for that reason.

And, continuing to generalize, I will hold that the middle class produces civilization because it is the only class constantly trained to come to a conclusion, poised as it is between the depth and height. It is not rich enough to have everything, nor poor enough to have nothing—and has to choose: to choose between a succulent table and a fine library, between travel and a flat in town, between a car and a new baby, or a fur coat and a ball dress: it has enough of the superfluous to give it freedom from necessity, but only through the constant use of discrimination: its life therefore is one long training of the judgement and the will. This by itself need not manufacture greatness; but it is the soil in which it is possible to make it grow. And for this reason, when the rich become too rich and the poor too poor, and fewer and fewer people live under the constant discipline of their decisions, the age of greatness withers. To produce the lifelong stimulus of choice both in thought and action should be the aim of all education, and the statesman ought above all things to provide a government that remains in the hands of people whose life has trained them in the inestimable art of making up their minds.

This happened, more or less, in Rhodes through the 4th century and the Hellenistic age that followed, when the citizens produced as near an approach as any in the ancient world to the welfare state. Their government, not called a democracy, remained in the hands of the well-to-do, who were yet bound by a system of 'voluntary' payments which provided for the maintenance, education, and enjoyment of the poor. In the fleet, in time of war, the rich men paid the crews, and expected the state to reimburse them when the danger was past; and the Rhodian ships beat those of Mithridates by six to twenty-five. The fighting men were citizens; the sailors and rowers may have been so also. A Rhodian gentleman would begin his career as a private soldier in the fleet; and their officers and men appear together in the dedications (as they do indeed in all the military inscriptions of the Hellenistic world). The general civilization of the city was carefully guarded by an elected bureaucracy that cared for public libraries and health and even manners—forbidding applause in public spectacles, or unnecessary running in the city streets. And the contentment and stability of the state were such that in the time of Demetrius' siege Rhodes dared to arm her slaves.

Prosperity

Such was the city that wrote the name of 'the Free Rhodians' on her coins—the clearing-house of the East when, in the 4th century, the close of the Persian wars again allowed trade to flow; the emporium for the Egyptian, Italian and African corn; the centre of banking; whose enduring link with our own history is that she too was once the 'protector of those who use the sea'.

Nor was there any symptom of decay when the prosperity of Rhodes was interrupted by the general misery that first followed the advent and, later, the decline of Rome. The Romans made Delos a free port and injured the Rhodian trade; but the causes of her decrease were more general. They lay in the loss of markets when the Aegean prosperity was broken, and in the Roman demand for slaves which tolerated, for over a hundred years, the piracy that provided them. And when the Empire brought a return of well-being, Rhodes revived. In 189 B.C., when Antiochus III was beaten, the Roman victory had been determined by the Rhodian command of the sea, and the city was given nearly all the coast from the Maeander to the Chelidonian promontory as a reward.[9] From this mountainous district—as well as from the Cretan mercenaries—she drew her soldiers. Along this Rhodian coast we were now sailing, making first for Marmaris and then for Caunus, which had been bought by the republic from the Ptolemies before the Romans came.

* * * *

The bay of Marmaris, so enclosed that it looks like a lake with hilly shores, is large enough for the whole British Mediterranean fleet to rest in; their summer sports have occasionally been held here—which caused us to be received in a matter-of-fact way in the little town of less than a thousand houses, that looked as if nothing more recent than a crusader could have tied up under the castle walls.

The evening was falling. Women were carrying amphorae

on their shoulders to fill at the pump near the shore. They wore the charming old-fashioned clothes—full trousers under a short skirt, and striped head-shawls wrapped tightly round the chin; and when they had filled their earthenware jars, they turned, with flat-soled, laden walk, up the flagged street to the castle that held their whitewashed cottages in its brown shell.

The pump was modern. In small lanes branching from it, oil lamps in tin cases began here and there to glimmer. A lute twanged its falling notes. The shops with their scanty variety of things for country use, glass, earthenware and iron mostly, a few bright-flowered cottons, a few bits of harness, were putting up their shutters, and men were playing backgammon in the café under the plane trees that made their square. On the sea front a new pier was visible to the imagination: heaps of cement lay waiting beside the marble shaft of a broken column to which *Elfin* was tied; and a statue of Atatürk looked benignly across pits where some pessimistic palms were trying to survive. There is a hotel in Marmaris; a *Kaymakam* lives in his residence; and a daily four-hour bus goes to Muğla, the head of the province, whence another six hours were said to take one on to Datcha: so short was the cut overland compared to our coastal voyage. One can go by taxi to Muğla, they said, in one and a half hours. Marmaris is in touch with the world, for all its lost appearance in the pocket of its bay.

Next morning early, on the 9th of October, we continued to coast south, until suddenly a fortified acropolis appeared among the wooded hills. This was Caunus, a place where Herodotus called the ancient people 'children of the soil', though they said themselves that they came from Crete.[10] We knew nothing much about them, and the business there between Tissaphernes and the Spartans, and Conon's blockade, were not in our minds. All we saw was the acropolis with a medieval wall; and D. B., having looked at it carefully through the

The swamp

glasses, turned to watch me putting on my shoes to disembark. He looked preoccupied.

"No one," he remarked, "could get across that swamp."

A reedy expanse with rushy edges bleached by the sun spread across about two miles of estuary to the slopes of thorny and uncultivated hills. The acropolis rose in apparent solitude some miles inland. Apart from it, there was no human sign in the landscape, except an automatic lighthouse winking its flame in the sunlight on a rocky islet in the still and shallow estuary bay. A red and black boat with two fishermen, and a hut with three soldiers were there in the foreground, interested in our manœuvres. We could not go up the river, said they, because of a sand bar at its mouth.

"What a pity," said I. "We must walk."

D. B. keeps his arguments for the reasonable. In the presence of unreason, he finds some other way, and I have never made up my mind whether this endearing quality is the result of his training in matrimony or religion. He now pondered, and presently said that he thought one might coax *Elfin* over the sand bar. She drew only as much water as reached to his waist, and if he went ahead and felt where the current ran deepest, Hüseyin could make her follow.

I was charmed to think of *Elfin* as a dog, and Hüseyin—keeping his thoughts to himself—turned the engines over slowly while D. B. let himself down over the side. The water, with yellow ribbed sand beneath it, reached his waist with an inch or so to spare, and he made for the angle of the bay where the river showed a bluer swirl of current on the curve. With a quick turn of the wheel and one scrape we were over, in a deep, smooth-flowing stream among plumed ranks of reeds.

We had nothing to do but to follow its windings, till the reeds, that grew in water, thinned out, and the banks solidified, and wooden palisades appeared with a foot-bridge, the trap for grey mullet of which this was a *dalyan* or fishery. On the land beyond, now substantial cultivated meadow, a factory and sheds, and a row of modern workmen's dwellings came in sight. The river wound on to a small village of about a thousand inhabitants, hanging with heavy trees, like a Monet painting, over the water; the wooded hills closed it in gently, and caught the last sunlight in their boughs.

There were very few people about. In a week or so the sluices would be closed, and the fish whose grey forms were whirling like dim troops of Valkyrie beneath our keel, would be turned into a hundred and forty tons of salted mullet and four tons of the uninteresting red sort of caviar they keep in beeswax from hives in the pinewoods nearby. But at present the people were away, picking cotton on the shores of the inland lake to which our river led; and as the darkness crept towards the water, a caique dropped downstream bringing the women home. They filled the benches and sat on the gunwale, their heads wrapped in white like the women of Tanagra, but with a country solidity about them. The evening closed round them, trailing amethyst mists. We seemed far away from everything here, buried in mere life, an agricultural peace that has tucked up many civilizations more permanent than the Rhodian. Above the peasant women's boat, carved high up out of reach on the hillside cliff, were the pillars and pediments of our first Lycian tombs.

CAUNUS

Alexander's Road

There had been seen an eagle perching on the shores astern of Alexander's vessels . . . it meant (he thought) that he would beat the Persian fleet from the land.   ARRIAN, Anabasis I. 18, 6–9.

CAUNUS HAD NOT BEEN EXPLORED WHEN COLONEL LEAKE travelled about Asia Minor in 1800. It was discovered nearly forty years later by Mr. Hoskyn of H.M.S. *Beacon.*[1] It must have been difficult to reach and a death-trap from malaria through all the centuries that preceded the discovery of D.D.T. Strabo mentions the green complexions of the people, and quotes the man who called it a city where even the dead walk.[2] But it was a fine city, with a naval arsenal, and a deeper river, presumably, than now, accessible to ships. It and its harbour lie forgotten, and the black coot float among reeds where the great wall pours its stone down the hill to a square port tower. The swampy estuary chokes it, where then there must have been sea. Another river-port upstream may have opened out under the cliffs where the tombs are carved. The ruins of the city lie on the neck of land between them, under the acropolis with its mean medieval battlements, and washing up to the high hill behind it, which the city wall reaches.

Two tortoises were courting in the sun. D. B. and I, as we made our way through the tussocks of the burnet, heard a dry sound, like the stroke of a small hammer; and beside a bush we watched the duet—or rather a one-sided argument—which the male tortoise carried on with repeated blows of his shell, as hard as he could make them (his head drawn in out of the way), on the back of his companion, who was trying with every sign of boredom to walk away.

We went on up the hill, following the wall to a gate; its monolithic posts and lintel faced the empty bend that held the harbour. The river sprawled beyond to its estuary, as if written in light with a careless pen. In the lap of the wide landscape, small as pebbles, lay a handful of cultivated fields. In the swamp, a few cows were browsing. A heron flew by. It was as if man and his histories were not so much forgotten as absorbed into the activity of nature, spinning her world and its sunshine through the restful afternoon. As we descended, after an hour or so, we still heard the tortoise battering his road towards the female heart, and went to watch him: and a touching thing happened: for as she moved away, and he with his wrinkled neck pursued her, he *mewed* with a high and eloquent note of longing. They disappeared together, and the sound of hitting stopped on the hill.

Brambles, the prickly holly-oak and spiky thickets of acacia grew thick as we reached the ruins where the city streets once led. A Roman bath with brick outlines to its arches fed a tree on its high wall; near it stood a small temple, with four fluted engaged columns and a door between them. All here was hard to reach because of growing trees, and barriers of thorns laid to keep the cattle in small enclosures. We struggled, scratched and bruised, and lost ourselves and each other, and finally emerged over the blocks of a fallen scene into a grey stone theatre, roughened and mossed over by time. Between the seats and through the gangways, twisted olive shoots had pushed their way till their roots had grown hard and colourless as the stone, and their leaves threw a small life of moving shadows on the places of the spectators who once walked up in white gowns and holiday sandals from the streets and the harbours below. Surrounded like the sleeping princess with thorns and thickets, the scarce-visited theatre of Caunus held its gaiety, as if the pleasantness that has once been could live for ever. Its seats, which the wind has scoured and the lichens have patched with colour, show row upon row the curve which the workers in stone once fashioned, to accommodate the legs of the spectators, and lighten and beautify the whole. And though every trapping that belongs to man has vanished, and the trees and the weather are alone there, a difference exists between the theatre and the surrounding loneliness, a comfort of civilization, though all that ever made it has gone.

Herodotus says that the people of Caunus spoke like Carians, but had different customs to which they clung, and mostly imitated the Lycians, as their tombs show. Their chief pleasure was to gather together in companies and drink, men, women and children. They carried on a border warfare with Calynda—inland, on the cliff of a high hill which we passed on our return journey; and the Caunians once, when foreign creeds had been established among them, 'resolved to worship the gods of their fathers only; and put on their armour . . . and gave chase as far as the boundaries of Calynda, smiting the air with their spears; and said they were casting out the strange gods'.

Calynda must have been within reach of water somewhere, for its King commanded at least one ship under Xerxes, and was rammed by Queen Artemisia at Salamis in a rather unsporting way. We did not explore the boundaries, but followed the river some ten miles only to Lake Köyejiz— a strip eight miles by three, hidden behind the reaches that pierce the coastal hills and open out at Caunus. On its northern shore the main road passes that cuts the Turkish promontories on a short internal axis, used since the Lydian kings first consulted the snake-man of Telmessus to the present day, when that same southern port, which has changed its name from Telmessus to Makri and Makri to Fethiye, exports a yearly one hundred and fifty thousand tons of chrome. The road travels towards it without disrupting the solitude, and the modern cluster of houses at the head of the lake, though rich with tangerines and gardens, has still an untidy look, like a housewife who has not done with her morning business or settled into the routine of her day. Prosperity there must always have been among the watered wooded slopes that lie in their beauty between the high snows and the sea. Round the lake shores, now lined with maples, figs were grown which Caunus exported—whose vendor's cry in Rome, "Cauneas, Cave-ne-eas", was taken as a bad omen when Crassus set out for Parthia in 55 B.C.[3]

The main Southern Highway ran, as it still does, across the Anatolian plateau to the Cilicean Gates; and the more westerly route, crossing the Maeander into Caria and passing through Physcus (Marmaris) to the south, was always subsidiary, and difficult when it reached the Lycian hills. But it led through the forest lands that built the Aegean ships and provided sailors, and this was why Persian governors rode up and down it so frequently, when Aspendus in Pamphylia was the station for Tissaphernes' fleet and both Athens and Sparta were perturbed by the menace of its arrival in the north. 'By bringing up the fleet, he would in all probability have given the victory to the Lacedaemonians,' says Thucydides.[4] This naval influence of the south continued while timber-built ships were wanted; and inspired one of the most interesting decisions ever made by Alexander.

Arrian tells how, as soon as his successful storming of Miletus was accomplished, Alexander decided to disband his navy,[5] both from want of money at the time and also because his fleet was not strong enough to face an action with the Persians at sea; he had no intention to risk disaster with even a portion of his armament. He also reflected that, as he now held Asia with land troops, he no longer needed a navy, and that by capturing the Persian coast bases he would break up their fleet, since they would have nowhere to make up their crews, and, in fact, would have no seaport in Asia. He therefore marched towards Caria and—gambling on and neglecting the main line of his communications across the plateau (which remained a very weak link in his chain till after his death)—he turned into this mountainous side-route of the west and fought the inland campaigns that followed, so as to sap the Persian sea-power at its roots before ever the battle of Issus was fought. There can be few examples of risk more coolly and imaginatively taken. Cortez burning his boats might be a parallel, on the shores of Yucatan.

When Fellows rode about Lake Köyejiz in 1840, he saw the end of another régime—that of the Derebeys, who were being broken through the centralizing of government that followed the destruction of the Janissaries by Mahmud II. The father of the governor he met here had been 'a Derebbe of great power and importance; his house, which has now half of its quadrangle in ruins, would have accommodated many hundred dependents, and adjoining was another ruin of a large barrack. Ten ships of war, subject to his command, then floated in the lake'. But the power of the family was already extinguished, and Fellows, lodging in one of the apartments of the palace, found it half-ruined, although it then formed the whole village of Köyejiz.[6]

The work begun by the reforming Sultan still goes on, and the *Kaymakam* of Köyejiz now lives in a new village, with the amenities of life filling in, as it were, around him. The slowness of the change in the far and lonely landscapes shows how vast is the Turkish problem, now being tackled with gradual, steady perseverance.

We left Mehmet to explore and exploit this modern world, for food was running short again. *Elfin* meanwhile made a tour of the lake towards its north-east corner. A fine country house stood there with outlying gables rather Georgian, a

smoking chimney, and a grey minaret and low buildings beside
it, half-hidden in trees. It must have been built some time
late in the last century, and we hoped that the Derebeys had
settled and remained prosperous under the new dispensation.
In the foreground, on an islet, was the ruin of the church
described by Fellows, with five or six cottages of Greeks of
whom nothing now but the name, Jaour Adasi, and tumbling
walls are left. And it was pleasant, after more than a hundred
years, to recognize the landmarks of the best and, in many
places, the only Lycian traveller. The schisty limestone hills
were there as he described them, well wooded from their tops
to the sea; the heath was ten feet high; the lilac and wild sage,
cistus, *salvia aethiopis*, candytuft and wild lavender were not
in flower, but their bushes were warm with the scents of summer; and the spaces between them, and all crevices of ruins
were overgrown with *urginea maritima*, a tall leafless squill
clustered with flowers, paler than asphodel.

Mehmet had not found much food when we landed to fetch
him. With a silent audience about him, he was sitting under
trees at the café spinning the long saga of his travels, and a
rather empty basket showed that the market hour had, as
usual, passed him by. He was meant to be a gipsy, and liked
to see the world for the pleasure of seeing it, and only the
necessity of producing some sort of a meal three times a day
made him think of food at all. When released from *Elfin* and
allowed to tramp with us over ruins, he became young again
with the strength of the Kurdish mountains where he was
born. He put up uncomplainingly with his bunk in the chaos
of *Elfin*'s kitchen. He liked it because it was moving—a
miniature where everything was buried under a number of
other things, within reach of his hand. Here, with a tiny sink
in front and the primus stove beside him, he concocted our
meals, telling his stories to himself for want of a better audience,
with his white hair so bristly that it never seemed to need a

114

brushing, cropped close at the back and high at the top of his narrow, Armenian head that looked as if it had been chopped out with a chopper. In Smyrna he lived with a married daughter and ran a little business of hiring tricycles to children, as well as nominally working in the Balfour household under general feminine disapproval produced by his wholehearted avoidance of work. Work, I suspected, he thought of as the prerogative of women, and my own complete idleness on board the *Elfin* was a discord in his ideas of the universal order. It was a pain to him to dust (which he did very rarely) while I sat merely writing in my note-book close by, or to have to knock when I happened to be dressing and the table and seat where I slept were about to be turned into the breakfast-room. But, when these ruffles had erased themselves, when D. B. held the wheel and Hüseyin was sleeping, and the coasts were slipping by across a steady sea, Mehmet would come to sit on deck. Then he would take up the inexhausted saga of his life, and tell how he had deserted from the army in the first world war, and walked for seven months across Anatolia from Erivan westward to the coast, and been hidden by a merciful woman in her cabin, and finally reached his parents in Stambul. Or he would go back to his childhood and talk of the hills of Kurdistan—and from that old grizzled shell a new Mehmet would appear, full of tender memories of those spring meadows and their flowers. His voice would become different and young, he would put the fingers of both hands together to express the ecstasy of his feelings, and one realized that behind all this dislike of polishing the brass there was a poet who was hungry to see the world and its wonders, and fed himself with their remembered glow. As I look back at our voyage I see that perhaps there was in all four of us a common quality that made it happy, for we were all, in our separate ways, travellers at heart.

There had been thunder with intervals of rain most of the

day, for the first and only time on our journey. Now, near evening, the clouds rose and were cut by a broken rainbow, and the sun sent shafts across the dark blue hills. As we dropped seaward again down the gorge, the air was filled with resin: we could tell the plants of the slopes without seeing them as each sent its perfume across the deck of *Elfin* in the night.

Next morning, in fine weather again, we slipped out through the palisade of the fishery to the estuary bay. But the wind which had brought the rain had also heaped the sand-bar, and even the bay's glassy surface was filled with choppy waves. Hüseyin steered gloomily, looking for an outlet, and when none was apparent, D. B. decided to cast the anchor out beyond the bar and winch the *Elfin* through. This was desperately harrowing, as every wave lifted her while she laboured, and thwacked her on the ground.

"Nothing matters while she's on sand," D. B. called out as he pushed in the water. But Hüseyin, who was overboard in his clothes, looked as if a favourite daughter were being strangled, and I felt a human pain with each blow of *Elfin*'s neatly-painted bottom on the floor. It was over and she was through in a few minutes, with clouds of sand whirling about her. The whole operation had taken one and a half hours, and we were out in the open sea.

The wind had veered to the south, which is the exposed quarter of all this coast. It whitened a long smooth swell and wrapped, in mists that shone like silver, the far landscape where the Dalaman river pours down from its hills. Rocky islets with grassy caps were dotted here and there in the vast bay. One of them had a brick-built ruin upon it—a Roman pharos we guessed, but were too anxious about the wind to try to land.

The sun shone, the hours passed, the bright swell carried us past the bay and round the prongs of the headland of Lide, whose milky snouts sheltered water dark as night in the white arms of day. We bathed and went on, looking for the ruins of Lide but not seeing them. These were no longer the Grecian coasts where acropoleis lie close to the sea: the Lycians liked to build high in their hills.

We came close in now. The fjords held rich solitudes of trees that had grown as the soil had fed them, empty of men. The evening scents came to meet us as they had come from the slopes of Caunus, as if incense had been scattered on the air. Beside the last of the Lide promontories we turned into an inlet protected by two wooded islands. A little boat was there in the dusk, in green shadow, watching its nets in the water, whose floating gourds our furrow tilted here and there. Next morning we saw a small hamlet on a ridge: but now, nothing seemed near us but the dark. The trees and water slipped together; the sky ceased to be reflected; the only sound was the splash of our anchor falling. A few landing stones near a ruined hut showed pale in a clearing. Maples and pines had crept up to it, and it had ceased to belong to men. Here *Elfin* rested, like a firefly cosily lighted with our supper cooking inside her, while the darkness pressed upon her, with soft and mothlike wings.

Next morning, we fished round the inlets of Lide. D. B. tossed a drop of beer over the side in honour of Poseidon, and was rewarded with two *vlachos* and a *sinagrida* for our breakfast. When these had been dealt with, we made south to where another and a greater bay opened on to Strabo's Daedala of the Rhodians. There the Lycian shore began. The little port of Fethiye, the ancient Telmessus, is still the centre for the whole of this district of the south.

12

XANTHUS

The Lycian Federation

She sings like a swan beside the yellow streams of Xanthus.
ALCMAN, Lyra Graeca, I. 59.

Why have the sons of Priam
Received each his portion in chambers of quiet earth,
When reasonable words could have solved the quarrel for Helen?
EURIPIDES, Helen.

M AKRI VECCHIA, CALLED THE ISLAND OF SNAKES, LIES A little distance from the shore in Fethiye Bay. It has a fortress with walls that are like old teeth, worn to their gums with age, and olive trees hide them. Picnickers go there in summer and the snakes have departed—but the name recalls the magic practices of Telmessus, whose snake-men were seers in ancient Anatolia long before the days of Cicero and Pliny.[1]

The Lydian Meles sent for them before the reign of Croesus, and walked a lion by their advice around the walls of Sardis; and to Telmessus, according to Arrian, came Gordius, seeking an oracle, disturbed by the sight of an eagle that had settled on the yoke of his oxen as he ploughed. Passing by a village where a girl was drawing water, he told her his story, and— since the women and even the children of Telmessus possessed the prophetic gift—she advised him to return. She went with him, they sacrificed to Zeus, and married; and their son Midas was the first of the Phrygian kings. The knot which had tied the yoke of his father's oxen where the eagle alighted became the Gordian knot which Alexander is said to have cut.[2]

When Alexander, in the course of time, came to Asia Minor,

he took with him as his seer Aristander of Telmessus, who wrote a work on prodigies, and followed him to the Indus, and interpreted his dreams. Another Lycian too is heard of at this time, even more surprisingly adventurous, for he was able to become an interpreter to the army in Scythia.[3]

The story of Gordius shows that feeling for a sacred quality in women familiar in the Anatolian past. From it the Lycians derived their matriarchy, though their other customs were partly Cretan and partly Carian: for 'this one custom they have peculiar to themselves and agree therein with no other men, that they call themselves after their mothers and not after their fathers. . . . And if a woman of the citizens dwell with a bondman, the children are held of good birth'.[4]

Rich and remote, well skilled in archery, and strong in battle, the Lycians appear in the *Iliad* led by Glaucus who traced his descent through Bellerophon from Argos and exchanged his gold armour with Diomedes for bronze; and by Sarpedon, the son of Zeus and Europa and bravest of the Trojan allies, who remembered, far from eddying Xanthus, his wife and infant son. They held 'a great demesne by the banks of Xanthus, of orchard land and wheat-bearing tilth'; and both together 'went straight forward, leading the great host of the Lycians'.

Apollo Loxias was the lord of this land, to which he is said to have brought Hecuba after the fall of Troy.[5] And Olen the Lycian invented the hexameter in his honour, or so it is supposed, bringing it in hymns to Delos.

In those early days, so long as Sarpedon ruled in Xanthus, the people were called Termilae in the south and Troes in the north[6] where Pandarus ruled them, who also comes to us with still untarnished name from Lycia, 'Lykaon's glorious son, Pandarus, to whom Apollo himself gave the bow'. Of all the heroes in the *Iliad*, he appears most knowledgeable about horses, and recognized Diomedes by them in the press of

battle, and refused to drive those of Aeneas lest they might go
wild for the lack of their master's voice. He spoke of his own
with affection, in Lykaon's halls, champing white barley and
spelt beside their chariots, where Lykaon the aged spearman
charged him at his departing to mount horse and chariot to
lead the Troes: but he disobeyed, sparing the horses, 'lest in the
great crowd of men they should lack fodder that had been
wont to feed their fill'. It is a pity to remember Pandarus
unkindly; I prefer to think of him at Pinara, where the Lycians
still honoured him in Strabo's day, and where we climbed in
his memory through the recesses of Cragus.

Lycus the son of Pandion began the Lycian name, when he
came from Athens to Sarpedon and the Termilae; and from him
the 'Lycian' Apollo and the Lyceums of the world are derived.[7]

These legends suit Telmessus, a prosperous little town whose
history lies around it as wide as its own expanses of sea and
hills. It is difficult even now to think of it as a commercial
harbour that exported corn and wine to the Negropont
through the middle ages. In 1818, in Captain Beaufort's day,
it was the embarkation point for travellers from Istanbul to
Egypt. 'Small vessels,' he says, 'are therefore always found
in this gulf';[8] and they are still there, crossing its glassy spaces
—rusty and weatherbeaten steamers from many countries,
collecting chrome at unobtrusive jetties, out of the way of the
main street of Fethiye, where *Elfin* tied up to an empty quayside by the café, and D. B. met the officials and his friends. The
old commerce, timber and tar and cattle, salt and firewood,
which went to Rhodes, was still represented by stacks of tree-
trunks sawn in lengths and waiting; and two caiques, one from
Alexandria and one from Syria, were anchored ready to load
them in the bay.

From this time, travelling southward, we met no more
steamers: the small fortnightly packet that calls at the tiny
harbours missed us, and the sailing ship alone—with the help

of oil—passed in her ancient tracks. The sight of her was a constantly repeated delight, for she moves naturally here in her own seas—not intrusive, like the steamer that arouses, however small, its own commotion—but as if she were the climax of a world that has made her, a part of forests whose trees her masts remember, whose boughs sing songs echoed from mountain gaps on narrow winds. The voice of the waves is woven with her timbers, so that only a sailor can tell which is the ship's voice and which is that of the sea. When I looked that night from the port-hole of *Elfin*, the Egyptian caique was picked out by the harbour lights and rode with shining painted bows on the soft dark arms of the water; the Syrian boat near her was caught in profile. She showed the long yard-arm that prolongs the prow and gives a look of the beaked galley to these peaceful travellers of today. She rode, isolated as a dew-drop, under a green flag with the crescent upon it; her polished stern bound with an Arabic name—*Slave of the Almighty*—and the moon-date of the Muslims carved in a wreath of foliage. One oil-lamp on the empty deck lit the base of her masts and shrouds that climbed into the blueness of the night.

On land, above the narrow line of the town at the water's edge, the patched walls of a fort hold the low rise. A mountain climbs behind them, and Lycian tombs look out from the face of a cliff.

The main goal of our journey had been the sight of these tombs. They are clustered over all the rock citadels of their district, and nowhere, apparently, outside it; and in their three or four different patterns they reproduce barns and houses that can still be seen in remoter valleys, though fast disappearing.

They are carefully illustrated by Fellows, whose book tells of the discovery and removal to the British Museum of the marbles from Xanthus, and describes their various types. The sarcophagus is mounted on blocks of stone; its roof was once covered with skins whose heads perhaps decorated the gable and originated the akroterion? This Lycian ogee is said to come from the shape of a hull, or from the natural twist of pine boughs that made a curving line; together with the mortising of the wooden beams, that intersect and fit into each other at the corners, it is peculiar to Lycia. All the detail of the wooden pattern is preserved in stone, and the flat roofs of modern cottages, where ends of tree-trunks protrude and support a top dressing of earth, are carved in the older tombs. In later models, these ends of tree-trunks are squared under a pediment and become known as the dentil. Travelling down the ages, they show the Lycian ghosts behind Palladian villas and all that has followed in the west.[9]

The people's history is written in the mixed types. The forest dwellers added the idea of small temple façades of the Ionian pattern to their wooden structures. There was Attic influence in Xanthus as early as the 6th century, and in 446–5 B.C., in a contribution to the confederacy of Delos, the Hellenism of Lycia was evidently recognized.[10] If I were a Turk, I should treasure these records; they show the very stuff that Turkish history is made of, the solid foundations of old Anatolia leavened to so many purposes by the movements of the trade routes and the coasts. Nor need they fear for the credit of their mainland. 'It was the narrow strip of shore that was magnetized by the greater mass of the interior, and the Achaeans parted with many of their characteristics under the new conditions . . . In such ways they reached the perfection of the temple of Athena Nike and the Erechtheum, which were not so much the works of their particular architects as the matured fruit of a succession of harvests: the result, as we see now, of the dispersion to Asia, of the atmosphere which the Asiatic colonist breathed, and of the Archaic temples of the east.'[11] Professor Dinsmoor explains the meaning of history more authoritatively than I can—a fruit of harvests for which no race or people or nation has scattered the seed alone.

Lycian tombs and ruins

Apart from this teaching, the Lycian cliff tombs eventually become rather dull. There are so many of them, and they are very much alike, and there is nearly always a great deal of uphill walking to reach them. The day came when D. B. and I looked at each other and asked: "*Must* we go up and look at that tomb?" For unlike the sailing boat that still has all the unexpected around it—the world for which the Lycian carved his stone so carefully is dead. From their empty and pillaged grave-chambers cut in the rock-face of Fethiye, the Ionic pillars and pediments, the elaborate doors with their petrified knobs and architraves and panels, look out blankly: the almond trees that shed their yearly blossom among untidy little houses below them have the secret which they have no longer—the happy secret of being alive.

The historian, however, gathering his evidence as if he were blowing on ashes, comes here and there upon some ember which still keeps its fire; and one might as well go blindfold as travel through a country like Asia Minor without preparing oneself with some part of this rewarding drudgery to make the landscape quicken in one's sight. The mere sound of names familiar through the ages adds beauty. Massicytus or Cragus become easy names on either side of the Xanthus valley, that drops between them from pastoral uplands of little towns now melted into earth. Oinoanda, Bubon, Balbura—from them the river works through its gorges to the lowland reaches, 'the wheat-bearing tilth', where the olive trees stand in corn as if it were water, and the blonde stream flows between parklands that might be England, or shadowed under maple banks and pines.

There, some eight miles from the sea, the ruins of Xanthus hold a low acropolis which the river half embraces; and there the Xanthians twice destroyed themselves in sieges, first holding out against Harpagus and the army of Cyrus, and later against Brutus and Rome. For when Harpagus, in the middle of the 6th century, had defeated the Carians of Pedasum in the interior (whose priestesses used to grow a beard in time of trouble), he came down into the plain of Xanthus, and 'the Lycians fought few against many and ... when they were put to the worse, they gathered ... their women and their children and their possessions and their servants ... set fire to all the citadel, and ... issued forth and all died fighting. And the most part of those who now say they are Xanthians are strangers, except four-score families ... who chanced to be abroad at that time and so were saved. Thus Harpagus got Xanthus; and in like manner he took Caunus also; for the Caunians mostly imitated the Lycians'.

When centuries had passed and the city had recovered, the Roman civil war harrowed the lands of Asia, and Brutus came to Xanthus. He was, whatever Plutarch may say, an unlovable man who starved his debtors and lent money at 48 per cent, and made his wife kill herself to live up to him, apart from murdering Caesar. 'He sent to the Lycians to demand from them a supply of money and men and ... surprising them as they were eating, killed 600 of them, and afterward, having taken all their small towns and villages round about, he set all his prisoners free without ransom, hoping to win the whole nation by goodwill. But they continued obstinate, taking in anger what they had suffered, and despising his goodness and humanity; until, having forced the most warlike of them into the city of Xanthus, he besieged them there. They endeavoured to make their escape by swimming and diving through the river that flows by the town, but were taken by nets ... which had little bells at the top, which gave present notice of any that were taken in them. After that, they made a sally in the night, and seizing several of the battering engines, set them on fire; but being perceived by the Romans, were beaten back to their walls, and there being a strong wind it carried the flames to the battlements of the city with such fierceness that several of the adjoining houses took fire. Brutus, fearing lest the whole city should be destroyed, commanded his own soldiers to assist and quench the fire.

'But the Lycians were on a sudden possessed with a strange and incredible desperation; such a frenzy as cannot be better expressed than by calling it a violent appetite to die, for both women and children, the bondmen and the free, those of all ages and of all conditions strove to force away the soldiers that came in to their assistance from the walls . . . Brutus, extremely afflicted at their calamity, got on horse-back and rode round the walls, earnestly desirous to preserve the city, and stretching forth his hand to the Xanthians, begged them that they would spare themselves and save the town. Yet none regarded his entreaties, but, by all manner of ways, strove to destroy themselves; not only men and women, but even boys and little children, with a hideous outcry, leaped into the fire, others from the walls, others fell upon their parents' swords, baring their throats and desiring to be struck. After the destruction of the city, there was found a woman who had hanged herself with her young child hanging from her neck, and the torch in her hand with which she had fired her own house.

'It was so tragical a sight that Brutus could not endure to see it, but wept at the very relation of it and proclaimed a reward to any soldier that could save a Xanthian. And it is said that only 150 were found, to have their lives saved against their wills. Thus the Xanthians, after a long space of years . . . repeated by their desperate deed the calamity of their forefathers, who after the very same manner in the Persian war had fired their city and destroyed themselves.'[12]

Herodotus describes them in the army of Xerxes, armed with corslets and greaves, hooks and featherless arrows from the reeds of the Xanthus marshes, and bows of that cornel wood which made the spears of Asia Minor better than those of the

Greeks until the Macedonians came. The walls, for which the Lycians were ready to fight so desperately, are shown in one of the tombs of Pinara and reproduced by Fellows, with their battlements and gates and the long-haired[13] sentries before them.

Here, according to Fellows, is the most beautiful landscape in the world, and I would not gainsay him. D. B.'s Land Rover had come from Smyrna overland to meet him, and took us through grasslands from Fethiye until, at the twenty-first kilometre, we turned south into a country road. Here Xanthus ran between harvests of maize and sesame in and out of sight on our left. On the higher ground, sloping bays drop from the defiles of Cragus, under glades of the palamut oak—*quercus Aegilops*—or through those Lycian pine groves whose boughs bend more easily and drink the sunlight more richly than any other pines. And when we came to Minara, which is at an hour and a half's walk from Pinara at the foot of its ravine, we found the village as Fellows describes it, a handful of cottages climbing one above the other in a tangle of pomegranate, olive, pear and almond trees, with aubergines grown huge like creepers, and tangerines, lemons and quince, thick as a jungle; and myrtle and *agnus castus* just breaking into flower.

Not many travellers can have come here since Fellows' first visit a century ago, and half the village evidently meant to escort us up their hill. The schoolmaster, who had never himself explored the ruins, decided to take us. One of the oldest inhabitants, unable to climb so far, gave him instructions. With their babies or other bundles strapped to their backs, the women stood around, ready to smile and talk if asked to do so. They had that remarkable Turkish solidity which the ancient Anatolians so rightly discerned as a basic feminine characteristic, and they were graceful in spite of it, under the full red trousers and bright short skirts and tightly-buttoned bodices in which they work all day.

Pinara

I would quite readily have lingered to make the acquaintance of the village, having long ago discovered that solitude is a luxury hardly ever to be enjoyed in the wilder parts of Asia. But D. B. is all for landscape undiluted and hates to have his ruins messed up with people. Having asked for a guide, he walked on in a resolute insular manner, evidently hoping that the little straggling procession that followed might be ignored into non-existence.

Far from it. They were delighted to see how like a pasha he strode ahead, leaving the harim with her poor Turkish to deal with conversation as best she could. She was intrigued by tortoises, who were creeping about the lettuces. "They eat our gardens," the people said. "They do us damage. But how can we help it? One cannot chase them if they come as guests."

Charmed with this, and with the coins that the small boys brought—a mixture of Hellenistic, Roman, Byzantine and a penny of Edward VII—I could have wished the schoolmaster away. His education was making the shepherds and peasants who knew the way quite dumb, and I thought very little of a young man who complained of the dullness of life and had never seen his own antiquities.

The site of Pinara meanwhile grew higher and more majestic before us as we climbed. A round tower of rock, from which it gets its name, was pitted like a honeycomb with tombs, and ruins lay in heaps on a flat ledge below, throttled in thorny scrub. Across an easy neck of land we reached a slope where the theatre nestled, hidden and stuffed with trees but with stone seats and side ramps intact, and an arch and door of the proscenium standing. The river, tumbling from behind the great acropolis over white boulders, in the shade of sycamores, came curving round agora and theatre hill, and gnawed the once-inhabited slopes: for Pinara has fallen back to wildness. Wolves, jackal, wild boar, bears, deer and panther still live in its forests; and no place could show the difference more clearly, between the hill citadels loved by the Lycians and Carians, and the easy sea approaches of Ionia.

We climbed steep ledges into a few tombs, with Lycian inscriptions and some traces of the red and blue colour on the letters that Fellows mentions; but the famous bas-relief escaped us. A cast of it is in the British Museum, and that perhaps made it seem less necessary to scratch oneself with thorns: or the vastness of the place with its cliffs and valleys and innumerable tombs overcame us; and the afternoon was upon us and Xanthus far away. I should have liked to spend some weeks in these high glades and walk about their ruins: as we moved down, a door quietly opening seemed to close again and a longing to return remains with me. But we left the high Lycian fortress and descended, and said good-bye to Minara, and, following the bays of the valley by an uneasy track, left the gorge that leads to Sydima, another of the Lycian towns, and kept straight on, to Kestep in the main valley. A müdür came out here, and gave us a policeman escort. New houses were building, and little girls with books under their arms and brightly-printed clothes and neat white collars were trooping out from school. An atmosphere of prosperity was about.

The road now went easily, under woods, through afternoon shadows and slanting lights, across the river by a wooden bridge to where in the dusk the acropolis of Xanthus held the way to the sea. Fellows had found that one hut and two barns constituted the whole city, and had camped with no signs of life but the footsteps of wolves, jackals and hares, near the river. He describes it as one of the most powerful, wild and unmanageable streams, and it did indeed drown two of the British sailors. But he stayed for two months, and built a camp immediately beneath the city ruins. Here cricket was perhaps for the first time played in Lycia, and here we in our turn found three of the kindest of French archaeologists, MM.

Demargne, Metzger, and Prunet, surrounded by all their treasures ready packed to leave in two days' time.

They gave us a share of their dinner, agreeable conversation, and room for camp-beds in their kitchen, which was the only shelter they had apart from a room where they and their antiquities slept together upstairs. Very few and small cottages have scarcely interfered with Fellows' solitude, though the swamp is dwindling and cultivation spreading through the valley.

The Harpy tomb, from which the sailors of H.M.S. *Beacon* took the British Museum friezes, is as they left it—so precarious now with its makeshift supports of crooked pine boughs that Professor Demargne was planning to renew the scaffolding. Together with another tomb it stands on the acropolis beside the theatre, near a late colonnaded agora and fountain, of which the earthenware conduits only are left. The city renewed itself again and again. Its necropolis stretched to the east, and Hellenistic and later suburbs lay still unexcavated, on the south-west slope below us, where a Hellenistic archway showed the old road up the hill.

In the 5th century A.D. Xanthus was famous for her schools. One of her bishops sat in the council of Nicaea; and the foundations of a church on the acropolis are there, on the edge as it were of the city's final crumbling. The Nereid monument, built nearly a thousand years before,[14] stood on the skyline, as one climbed towards the gateway from the plain.

To the north, behind the agora, is the great stele, the longest Lycian inscription yet known, and not yet deciphered except for two references to news mentioned by Thucydides, that fix its date to 428–418 B.C. Seven hundred years and more of building must have looked down on the river in the later days of Rome; the great century of Hadrian showed its activity here as in most of the Levant, and the 2nd century B.C. too was a busy time for masons. Before this, Alexander came from Halicarnassus, received the surrender of Telmessus, and crossed the river to Xanthus, where Pinara and Patara and thirty smaller strongholds submitted, while the envoys from Phaselis were travelling up from the south to crown him with a golden crown.[15] Xanthus then must have been small but beautiful, the Nereid monument new in its cluster of statues, and the wall, that had been rebuilt after the Persian destruction, showing its polygonal stones not as today in small but precious fragments, but in all their armed beauty along the city height.

Ashes have been found under the 6th century ruins to confirm the Persian burning, together with many ceramic shards of Athenian ware to prove the activity of commerce with Greece in early days. As we walked with Professor Demargne among the far-scattered tombs of the hillsides—carved here and there with dancing figures of the Greek or lion-bull fights of the oriental—the lost or weathered outlines came to life, and the love of the Xanthians for their city and their death with its destruction seemed as natural as the sharp scent of the thyme, quivering about us in the sun.

Something of all this expense of spirit remains. In their smallness and remoteness, the Lycians too made their discoveries, and one of them was the way to live in peace together by a system of proportional representation. Their league lasted from before the coming of Alexander through the wars of the Ptolemies into the Roman age, until the Senate put an end to it by annexation, in A.D. 43. In the days of its effectiveness, twenty-three cities assembled, and each of the largest (Xanthus, Patara, Pinara, Olympus, Myra and Tlos) commanded three votes; those of intermediate importance had two, and the rest one; and they contributed, in the same proportion, to taxes and other public charges. The people, says Strabo, were not inclined to violence: their country, 'difficult and rugged with good harbours' was not used to produce or shelter pirates nor—as at Side in Pamphylia—were the free-born prisoners sold in their streets by notice of the public crier. 'But the Lycians continued to live as good citizens, with so much restraint upon themselves . . . that they were never influenced by the desire of base gain, and persevered . . . according to the laws of the Lycian body.'[16]

In the wars of Alexander's successors, the Ptolemies tried to bring them into the financial bureaucracy of Egypt. Garrisons were billeted, fodder for the horses demanded, new taxes added. Letters have come down describing an increase in the farming-out of the money-tax, a decrease in the gate-tax (chiefly on wine), and the lease of the revenue from purple, which brought in about £300 a year. Owners of orchards and flocks paid taxes, and the landowners a part of their crops; there is even a suggestion that a poll tax was paid in the 2nd century B.C.[17] Disentangling itself from such immediate concerns and the way in which they are dealt with, an *idea* sails out under whatever force has made it, into the universal stream. The Lycian, differing from the centrifugal Greek or even from the Carian, succeeded in keeping his little cities distinct and yet united, and will be counted among the unifying influences of the Alexandrine centuries before he too goes down into the melting-pot of Rome.

A decline came over all these valleys. Arab raiders caused it, and the break-up of Byzantium; the neglect of roads through hard mountain ranges; and—perhaps chiefly—the spread of malaria as population and cultivation diminished. Hidden behind this veil, the towns of the accessible flat lands disappeared, while the higher and healthier places lived on, and carried their brave and kindly character into a new language and a new religion. And they must have mingled easily, for the Lycian and the Turkish virtues are very similar. They belong to the great village world of Asia.

13

APERLAE

Loyalty and the Mercenaries

For who would desire a condition of things where pirates command the seas and mercenaries occupy our cities?

ISOCRATES, Panegyricus, 115.

Heroes are bred by lands where livelihood comes hard.

MENANDER, The Cousins.

IT WAS VERY PLEASANT IN THE LYCIAN VALLEY IN THE SUN. We drove the Land Rover from Xanthus to Patara, with care and success, between cotton and swamp, as far as the ground could hold us up, and found a Roman gate intact beside marshes long ago left by the sea. A little Corinthian temple, and baths and bits of wall are there with the reeds about them, and the harbour where St. Paul landed must have been presumably on the western side. It was the most important in Lycia, but not big enough to hold the united Roman and Rhodian fleets.[1]

On solid ground at the edge of the swamp to the west, were the long fine lines of Hadrian's granary, and temples or public buildings beside it, barrel-vaulted and carved, all filled with thickets of the scented bay. On the southern headland, near what we thought a lighthouse, and among dunes that have flattened themselves against it, is the theatre which a Q. Velius Titianus dedicated to his daughter in the time of Antoninus. All is buried except the higher auditorium on the side that the wind rarely reaches. And the whole of Patara, in the rankness of its fens and its decay, is sealed by the barrier of sand that has piled itself against it, and hides the estuary of Xanthus, and gives a foothold on its inner edge to the pines, that sing stiffly whenever the south wind blows.

A cottage inhabited the loneliness, where cows and goats were grazing. The Roman business that in its time submerged the legendary atmosphere of Lycia, so strong in the other towns, is now forgotten. Vessels no longer ply as tenders to the sanctuary of Leto and her children, and the city of the Xanthians beyond it;[2] the bronze bowl is lost or melted, which the Lycians thought that Hephaestus had worked on, ignorant as they were, says Pausanias, of the Samian bronze. St. Nicholas was born here,[3] but already long before, in the 1st century B.C., pirates were active and brigands had settled on the coast; and Mithridates had plunged white horses dedicated to Poseidon, into the long waves, sleek as ringlets, that break on the sandy shore.[4]

> or dov'è il grido
> Di quella Roma, e l'armi e'l fragorio
> Che n'andò per la terra e l'oceano?
> Tutto è pace e silenzio, e tutto posa
> Il mondo, e più di lor non si ragiona.

Yet one event must be remembered, falling on the Lycian beaches with a strange bell-like note as if it were an echo from the West. For Hannibal, defeated in Italy, became Antiochus' captain in these waters, against Rome. When their skill in 189 B.C. had beaten him, the Rhodians sent twenty beaked ships to Megiste (Castelorizo), and to Patara, while Eudamus, their admiral, was posted with the seven largest to Samos to urge on the Romans the capture of Patara 'with whatever wisdom and whatever influence he had'.

Hannibal dared not venture past Lycia, anxious though he was to join the King's Fleet and meet the Romans threatening in the north; and Antiochus fought and lost the battle of

Myonnesus without him; and having forfeited the mastery at sea which might have held up the Romans at the Bosphorus, abandoned all that region. He fought the war out on land and was vanquished; and the narrow sea-strip between Rhodes and Lycia had no small part in the final defeat of Asia and the triumph of Rome.

The *Elfin*—delayed by D. B.'s business among officials—saw Patara next day in twilight from the sea. She came swinging round Anti-Cragus, borne on waves that lifted her rhythmically, like oar-blades in the sun. Hamlets and single houses showed high on the coast above her. The inhabited shelf lifted in a steep slant behind them, to one of the eight peaks of Cragus, polished and naked in the sky. The slopes were red; the far mountains opened out, blue as if cut in lapislazuli; their snowless summits of white limestone were blunted and barren. A botanist, Mr. P. H. Davis, a friend of mine, has clambered in this region and written about the tombs of Telmessus. Their very slight degree of weathering, he says, through more than two thousand years, demonstrates 'the permanence of a saxatile habitat for plants'. Such a summary, for some reason, amused me—a long-delayed snub to the Lycians' careful and bourgeois carving for their dead.

The hills were now steep and furrowed; their blurred landscape was repeated in the water; and as we slipped along them, we came to St. Nicholas and his islets, sailing on their own reflections like rafts loaded with ruins, on a motionless sea.

Hüseyin knew St. Nicholas as a well-used refuge for sailors in bad weather, though it has no water, and only an animal or two grazes there now and then—brought across by boat, for no one lives on the island. Tombs, houses, Byzantine chapels and cisterns tumble one below the other to the edge. Their steps and boathouses, cut in the stone, are now a foot or two under the level of the sea, since all this coast has been subsiding.

Aegean bathing

A cloud—a wisp the size of one's finger—developed between D. B. and me, for I could not bear, and refused, to pass the island by. We were late, and were going to pick up the French archaeologists—mere reason as usual was on the consular side. But I was granted ten minutes on shore to see the lowest of the churches, and Hüseyin rowed me across, smiling—for what is time to him, who has the Aegean in his veins? And D. B., impressed, I hoped, by my honest rapidity but not saying so, allowed me twenty minutes more for a bathe when I got back.

The water was very deep. It held its light far down inside it like the star in a sapphire: its daily enchantment is never to be forgotten. For what words can give even the ghost of the Aegean bathing? When the body is lost because the radiance and coolness of the world have become a part of it, and nothing seems oneself any longer; and the warmth and light between two darknesses of atmosphere and sea, caress all that emerges —the imperceptible moving tide, and our shoulders, and the embracing mountains that burn above us on the noonday edge of their horizon, and in their slower cycle also carry as we do some fire at their heart. There in perfect solitude the pine trees hang over the white rocks and the water lifts us, alive and unresisting, through its own regions, from which a vast loom seems to be weaving sea and earth and sky, out of their basic unity into the varied loveliness of Time. And who can wonder that such hours gave light to the lives that contained them; or who would be mad enough to change them for any money that the world can give? No life is wasted that can remember them, as I hope to do till I have to leave it all. In the midday silence, in the immense semi-circle of woods and mountains, with the deep fjord in their lap and nothing made by man in sight except the island ruins, the little noise of *Elfin* stirring up her engines for departure, the sight of D. B. astride the deck, obviously thinking I would be late but not saying so out of kindness, gave a comfortable human warmth.

Aperlae

We brushed the island trees as we passed them and made south again; and, as dusk was already falling, opened once more the great Xanthian valley, saw the sunset light on Massicytus and the hills above the distant gorges, and—not more than fifteen minutes walk inland on a slope above a little river—the irresistible outline of the empty but intact fortress wall of Pydnai. D. B., who is far too human to be consistent and likes his ruins classical, thought there might just be time to look at it and catch the Frenchmen, as we had arranged, at Kalkan in the next bay. Hüseyin landed us on the sand; and by the river, which is only a few miles long but quite deep where it flows through marshes to its sand-bar, we were lucky to find a peasant washing himself at the end of his day. His grey pony, loaded with faggots, stood beside him. He showed a little wormlike path and we hastened, with the glow fading on the fine polygonal masonry of the fortress before us, whose complete circuit in its emptiness, with nothing but a ruined apse inside it, is still exactly as Fellows drew it when he visited this place, over a century ago.

Some three or four acres of ground are held in the naked enclosure, and one can climb the steps to the square bastion of the gate, and pass under towers on the wall by doors whose solid lintels and single blocks of doorposts might still watch half a dozen ages through. The battlements are not so old, and are strengthened with mortar, which is absent from the wall itself. On its broad top the sentinels walked on slabs of stone laid in easy tiers, like the steps of a stair, to follow the gradient of the hill.

From here one saw the bay, and the sand in a long sweep that hid Xanthus' mouth and Patara beyond it, and the mound of Xanthus city inland, with mists of the cultivated country, and foothills lifting towards the hills. A green sky repeated the colours of the marshy pools, and a planet shone with a few thin cloudy bars of gold attending. Under it the sea was rising with darkened rim to the evening wind.

French archaeologists

We were twenty minutes late for our meeting with the French archaeologists at Kalkan; they had left, thinking our lights those of the coastguard. We would start before dawn next morning and overtake them at Kash before they went farther on their way.

At 3.30 the *Elfin's* engines began to turn over, and I opened one eye to see Hüseyin wrapped in his old duffle coat settling at the wheel. One of the consolations of age, I thought as I looked at him—to acquire a face so furrowed that it can get up without damage at all times, and I went to sleep again as we moved out. We had seen only the high steepness of the houses of Kalkan, whose hills are too sudden for small craft to anchor near them with ease.

The French were at breakfast under a plane tree, beside a bronze bust of Atatürk on a tall pedestal, in the square of Kash which was once Antiphellus. Balconied whitewashed houses, like a Devonshire cottage street, went from it uphill to a Lycian sarcophagus with lion heads and an inscription and fine carved podium, under another plane tree at the top. It was still early: children were passing, neat with satchels and white collars; fruit and vegetables were spread along lengths of black cotton on the ground; and on the sea front camels crouched in circles while their burdens—chiefly timber—were weighed on scales held up by a pole that rested on two men's shoulders. Goat-hair pack-saddles received them, on crooked wooden frames shiny with age; and by nine o'clock they had all been taken to their mountain places by steep ways, while the men of Kash settled quietly to cards.

As for us, we had already visited their theatre—pure and Hellenistic, with no Roman vomitoria, and built up at the back with fine and simple stone: and had sailed into the harbour of the little island of Greek Castelorizo without landing, and seen its stricken streets, which the fire ate when the people had been carried away to safety by British ships in the war.

Aperlae

The wounded little town on its eroded hills has painted and rebuilt its houses round the harbour. It shows that gaiety with starvation which one may call—in the Greek nation as in the Arab horse—the 'endurance heart'. I can never think of Castelorizo without a stab as if someone had hit me, for we visited it again a year later, and it still wore the same clean look among its ruins, but with more houses closed and fewer people, as if the ashes had increased and the spark grown smaller at its heart.

Now we left it and moved on, the *Elfin* heavy in the water under so many passengers, but filled with a pleasant murmur of conversation, of experts and amateurs in harmony, enjoying the same things from different points of view. The most haunted coast of the world was opening its afternoon fans of light, its legendary emptinesses and shining promontories before us. The shore route followed by Alexander went inland here, and its hedge-hog outposts of limestone were honeycombed with fortresses—if one looked closely through the maquis—built chiefly when Alexander's successors were fighting for the seaboard for their ships.

In an age when there were no maps to speak of, how did they get their knowledge of the routes they would follow, in a country almost as solitary, and over roads even worse than now?

There must always have been an interest in geography among the sea-going peoples. Plutarch would have us see young men in wrestling grounds and old men in shops as early as the fifth century sitting in semicircles sketching the lie of Sicily and the nature of the sea around it and the havens;[5] and Alexander from his adolescence showed a geographical bent. When the Persian ambassadors reached his father's court, he asked the distances of places and the line of the roads through the upper provinces of Asia.[6] But, when his time came, the mercenaries, the most characteristic and important product of the 4th century B.C., must have given him most of his actual information.

Rise of the mercenaries

The first mercenaries we hear of came from the Carian and Ionian seaboard. They went in the 7th century to Egypt, and a Colophonian name is scratched among others on the leg of the Abu Simbel Colossus. Antimenides of Mitylene served Nebuchadnezzar; and Croesus the Lydian sent Eurybatus to the Peloponnesus to recruit among the Greeks. In the fifth century, the Arcadian hoplites appear—deserters to Xerxes, 'men that lacked sustenance and would be employed'. They fought for Pissuthnes the Persian in Caria in 427; and served both sides at Syracuse; and were the bulk of the Ten Thousand with Cyrus. Thirty years later they were able to say that wherever men needed mercenaries, none were chosen in preference to the Arcadian.

With Xenophon's *Anabasis*, the mercenary comes into his own. He coincides with the end of the Peloponnesian war, which made it easy to collect wanderers whose fields had been destroyed; and friendly relations with Persia now brought the mercenary in touch with those who had the money to pay him. One may remember that Athens, in the thick of the Sicilian campaign, could not afford to keep the Thracian auxiliaries and sent them back. The steep 4th-century rise of the hired armies is largely due to the Persian exchequer. Increasing distances too, at which campaigns were fought, and the development of military science especially in Sicily, made the expert essential in war.

Through the 4th century one can follow the gradual eclipse of the citizen army, up to 338 B.C. and the battle of Chaeronaea, where it died in its ranks as it stood. It was good in some later moments for the defence of its own walls, as in Rhodes—yet even this achievement became rare after improved methods of siege were invented. One can watch the generals turning from amateurs to professional soldiers—from Cimon and Alcibiades to Conon, from Conon to Chabrias, Agesilaus, Chares, Iphicrates. They still depend on and obey their city, but their armies have become weapons personal to themselves. They can discipline and punish in a way that was impossible to the citizen commander: Iphicrates put two of his captains to death and disarmed and dismissed their men, as an earlier Athenian never could have done.[7]   The poverty of the cities after the long war made the general independent; he often had to rely on his own resources if he wanted to see his troops not only paid but fed.   Chares, when short of funds, was sent for by the Persian Artabazus; his soldiers compelled him to go, and he received a present with which he was able to furnish his entire army with supplies: and this inspired the taunt of Demosthenes on mercenary armies, that take a peep at the city's war, and go sailing away, and the general follows, because he cannot lead without giving them their pay.[8]

The Sicilian tyrants based a new fashion in tyranny upon the mercenary, and many copied him, like Jason the Thessalian, who made trial every day of the men under him, leading them in full armour, 'both on the parade ground and whenever he is on a campaign.   And whomsoever among his mercenaries he finds to be weaklings he casts out, but whomsoever he finds to be fond of toil and fond of the dangers of war he rewards, some with double pay, others with triple pay, others even with quadruple pay, and with gifts besides, as well as with care in sickness and magnificence in burial'.[9]

It was a short step to Philip of Macedon, and a natural climax; for the mercenary depended on brilliant leadership for his existence, and his existence was a need of his time.   Towards the second half of the century, in revolts of Egypt or of Satraps, which continually occupied the Persian kings, success came to depend exclusively on the presence of heavy or even light-armed Greeks—so much so that, in 358 B.C., Artaxerxes the King tried to safeguard himself against revolution by disbanding the provincial governors' mercenary armies.   The satrap Orontes, being thus unprovided, and attacked when the professionals he had sent for had not yet reached him, drew up his native ranks with Greek interpreters and in Greek armour, and circulated a rumour of the mercenaries' arrival, and saved himself from attack.[10]

As the century went on, hard things were said of these people, whom Isocrates describes as the common enemies of all mankind, 'hireling soldiers who are better off dead than alive'. His is the settled citizen's point of view, whose life is disarranged by disorder—the point of view, in the last war, of well-to-do French or Italians towards the Resistance which continually threatened their private security. Their real, legitimate dislike, if they had known it, was not the young man hiding in the mountains or, in the days of Isocrates, the poorly paid trooper in his shifting camp—but war itself, which turns peace-loving men into these ways. For who were these mercenaries, if not peasant farmers who had been the constitutional backbone of the citizen armies, or exiles made homeless by some revolution, of whom over twenty thousand assembled at Olympia in 324 B.C. to hear the welcome news of their recall.[11]

It is noticeable that prosperity at this time is attributed, by anyone who writes about it, to the fact that some region had escaped invasion—Chios, Cos, Cyprus, Corcyra or Rhodes. They gave rich loot at their first raiding and then, if the wars revisited them, their fields untended fell into decay, and the owners, too poor to re-establish them, were forced to sell. By the middle of the century, in Attica, big farms were the rule instead of peasant holdings, and Aristotle wrote wistfully about ancient laws that kept a democracy of husbandmen together, and allowed none to own more than a certain quantity of land. Meanwhile the young went off: perhaps they sold their property to provide a marriage portion for their sisters, and went abroad with Iphicrates to Thrace, and made some money, and returned. Yet the pay was poor enough, until Alexander

stretched the East at their feet.   Four obols a day (about 6*d.*)
were allowed for a Peloponnesian League hoplite in 383 B.C.
—only slightly above the level reached by an unskilled slave.[12]
Few can have taken to soldiering from choice.

Out of these wages they bought their own food at the
towns where they stopped, or in the markets that attended an
army.

Lysistrata : Now in the market you see them like Corybants
      jangling about with their armour of mail.
    Fiercely they stalk in the midst of the crockery,
      sternly parade by the cabbage and kail.
Probulus : Right, for a soldier should always be soldierly.
Lysistrata : Troth, 'tis a mighty ridiculous jest,
    Watching them haggle for shrimps in the market place,
      grimly accoutred with shield and with crest.
Strategus : Lately I witnessed a captain of cavalry,
    proudly the while on his charger he sat,
    Witnessed him, soldierly, buying an omelet,
      stowing it all in his cavalry hat . . .[13]*

As for the sailors, their meal in the days of Thucydides was
barley cake kneaded with oil and wine.[14]   And one wonders,
not at the hardness of these homeless men, but that loyalty
survived amongst them and, in a life torn out of its roots,
built up a new, professional honour, which they usually maintained.

In the early time, at the turn of the 5th century, there was
no organized system of recruiting.   According to Isocrates,
the cities spent more on their gifts to the recruiting officers
than on their wages to the soldiers, while commanders went
around, like the Boeotian Coeratadas mentioned by Xenophon,
advertising themselves for employment.   The cities had trouble

*These were citizen soldiers but the background is the same.

too with the honesty of their generals, who were apt to ask pay for more troops than they had. But the coming and going grew easier as relations with Persia became closer, and the numbers of the mercenaries multiplied and their gathering centres were known. Rising from about twenty-five thousand at the beginning of the century, the average of men in service remained not less than fifty thousand from 350 B.C. onwards when the Egyptian wars employed them more and more. In 369 the Persian King sent his Greek agent to mainland Greece to promote a general peace there, so that he might recruit more freely;[15] the lands which provided the good soldiers became increasingly important into the Roman rule.

Among such, this southern coast of Asia Minor must have been counted, with a brave, poor, hardy people and forests of cedar, cypress and pine for ships. After Alexander's death, Eumenes of Cardia came there recruiting, and before that, in 350 B.C., the Greeks of the seaboard sent six thousand men to help the Persian King.[16] Many of the Rhodian slingers must have come from among the shepherds of the Peraea. Young men, like the Lycian interpreter among the Scythians, were probably found scattered everywhere in the Persian lands; and older men, returned to their thin mountain fields, would talk then of Media, Phoenicia and Babylonia as now, in the remotest Turkish district, one may hear some account of Korea or the United States. From such people, with the Greek language current between them, Alexander could learn without the teaching of maps.

But, for the inhabitants of the coast land, what difficulties were brought by his invasion! It added one more tangle to the loyalties, already so complicated, of Asia Minor.

The word *loyalty* is so black-and-white, so often misapplied, so double-faced and hard to recognize from one side to the other, that perhaps it would be better to leave it altogether out of use? Its presence is assumed, its absence blamed, with a partial and unreasonable passion—rarely the same for him who speaks and him who hears from even the most slightly divergent angle; and the fact is that the word is a collective, whose use with a singular meaning is almost without exception a mistake.

There is always more than one loyalty to be considered. Race, government, custom, origin, religion—one has to choose between them, and the problem is not a simple matter easily dismissed. We can illustrate it in the 4th century in Asia Minor with the story of Mentor the Rhodian.

He was a mercenary captain employed in 350 B.C. with four thousand of his soldiers by Tennes the King of Sidon against the Persian King. Tennes betrayed his own city and ordered Mentor to open the gate, and the Persians took Sidon, and destroyed it and Tennes too. Mentor with his troops went over to the victor. There was nothing very pleasant here though no disloyalty. And now the Persian army, with other Greek troops added, marched to the Nile at Pelusium, where Spartans in Egyptian pay opposed them, Greek against Greek.

The attacking mercenaries were under three captains, each with a high Persian officer attached. Nicostratus of Argos, in a brilliant battle among the canals and marshes, defeated Cleinias of Cos who was fighting for Egypt with five thousand of his men. The second Greek contingent, under the Theban Lacrates, settled down to the siege of Pelusium, whose garrison, abandoned by their King, sent envoys for surrender: and, sacrificing his prospect of booty, Lacrates promised to see them safely to Greece with whatever they could carry on their backs. Some of his Persian colleagues, who were beginning to pillage regardless of this promise, he killed, an action which the Persian King, with remarkable detachment, approved.

Meanwhile Mentor, commanding the third contingent with Bagoas, the most trusted of the King's men, had taken Bubastis and many other towns. He did this by policy more than force, promising a mild reception to deserters and ordering the guards to give them free passage through the gates; so that there was chaos in the fortresses, the Egyptians treating separately with Bagoas and the Greeks with Mentor; until the Greeks captured the Persian nobleman and Mentor rescued him (by a secret connivance with his men). On this precarious basis a firm friendship was established between the two chiefs, and Mentor's career was made. He saved the Greeks of Bubastis, and became a purveyor of troops for Artaxerxes, and Bagoas stood by him for the rest of their lives. The King made him Satrap of the Asian coast and supreme commander, and his Persian brother-in-law Artabazus and Memnon his brother, who had both been involved in a revolt, were pardoned for his sake. They came back from asylum with Philip in Macedonia, and brought eleven nephews and ten nieces, all of whom Mentor looked after and helped in their careers; and when he died in his governorship, his brother Memnon succeeded him and served the Persian King, and became Alexander's most dangerous opponent—a loyal Greek, though fighting on the other side.

The loyalties of Asia, however many and however divergent, had grown respectable with age; and the only way to supersede them—and indeed the only way to establish lasting empire anywhere—was and is to bring to a nation a pattern of civilization whose intrinsic merits it can feel to be better than its own. By this means, in the mind of Alexander and his successors as well as through their actions, the Hellenization of Asia was later accomplished, as it had been accomplished long before in the barbarian valleys of Caria and Lycia, where we were sailing.

These valleys now ran parallel with the coast and out of sight. Their mountain lines were fluid one behind the other in four unbroken ridges of stone. They were graded from trees to scrub and weathered rock from base to top; and the light alone made them beautiful. Their defiles hung luminous yet dusky; and the whole landscape held hardness at its heart.

The water too, near the land, was stained with shadows, while we floated down an oyster-coloured sound. We were among islands, and had the long backbone of Kekova—the ancient Cisthene-Dolichiste—on our right, and were winding between pale outcrops of rock with small Byzantine ruins. Presently the little town of Kekova, the ancient Aperlae, was there on its hill before us, as though, surrounded by the mother-of-pearl evening, the pearl itself appeared. No ripple, no voice, no movement disturbed it; its calm reflection, of tombs and Crusading battlements and arched Crusading windows, lay there elongated in the water, out of focus at the edge so that its outlines were jagged, as if broken spears of long-forgotten battles had fallen in the sea.

Three small blue boats were in a shallow haven whose quays and slips have sunk beneath the water. An old gun to tie up to, and a few ancient stones piled at random, made the landing stage. From it the houses climbed, scattered sparingly among olives, within walls that had grown loose for them like a garment; they led to a ridge where a Ptolemaic fort held one pinnacle, and the castle, Venetian or Genoese, the other. Its Ghibelline battlements, stormed no doubt during assaults and sieges, had been mended by Seljuk or Ottoman and in 1818 still enclosed some Turkish cannon.[17] They curved across the hill summit and half hid, even from the deck of *Elfin* as we neared them, the seats of a miniature theatre carved in the rock at the castle's foot. Fields spread below, on the inland side of the ridge, in level patches of bright harvested land; and everywhere, in the cliff under the acropolis, on the crest of the castle walls, pressed among houses or standing half in water where we landed, the tombs and sarcophagi were scattered, as if the meagre inhabitants of today were being invaded by their more numerous dead.

Kekova

There are now not more than thirty-five or forty families. Their harvest of parched wheat (or burgol) was spread on black cloths on the flat roofs, drying in the sun. And the women came out kindly, offering an egg, or a drink of muddy water from their goatskins—all that they had to give.

When we left, after some hours, the whole picture of Kekova was spread out in the sunset before us, painted in mortal weakness by poverty and time. It was disturbing and strangely satisfying. Any alleviation, or improvement would have seemed impertinent,—a contrast too startling to be borne. For a haunted loveliness was woven into these mean constituents and the dignity it gave them was not to be judged in terms of comfort. The visible world had chosen to build its own perfection out of the short-comings of the human material; and its frailty was not to be counted by success or value, but by this atmosphere of loveliness in which it lingered, beyond the realms of judgement, like the blind loyalties of men.

14

MYRA

The Fold

Men are called Greeks more because they have a part in our culture than because they come of a common stock.

ISOCRATES, Panegyricus, 50.

And when we had sailed over the sea of Cilicia and Pamphylia, we came to Myra, a city of Lycia.

Acts, 27. 5.

THE ONLY NAVAL CARE I HAD ON *ELFIN* WAS TO KEEP THE rope of the dinghy clear of the propellor when we backed in or out of our landings. Now, with six men about, I relinquished this responsibility and the rope instantly got involved. This is not to say that women do things better, for the rope was frequently forgotten; but luck was on my side. M. Prunet and D. B., with masculine delight in a crisis for its own sake, dived happily underwater, while Hüseyin, detached as a minor Aegean god, looked on. But by the time the dinghy and propellor were separated, *Elfin* showed signs of fatigue in her engines; she limped with plaintive splutters of one cylinder (or whatever it is that her motive power is based on); and we sympathized, seeing her burdened with so large a household single-handed. A night's rest, we thought, would do her good. She chugged lamely along to one of the innumerable inlets stored in Hüseyin's brain, threading among rocks opalescent as sea-shells in the evening light. Kekova's battlements in the west faded against mountains green and gold. Curved shadows flaked from our wake like lazy fish, through the pale satin water.

In a low creek, open to the sky, where nothing was visible but shallow limestone and thorns, we anchored for the night. The silence lay there on naked rock like the scabbard round a

148

sword—until it was strangely broken in the darkness by two boys rowing their little boat from Finike, asking for water as they hugged the shore. Before dawn we started, and in one and a half hours anchored off a hook of cliff which is the present approach to Myra, the modern Demre, whose estuary is now submerged in sand-dunes. Their ribbed wind-blown shoulders lifted themselves cold with dew out of the peaceful morning sea.

A four-roomed guardhouse, by a tiny platform at the water's edge, was the focus of such life as the vast landscape showed. Against its mountain background, camels were moving across the sand. Boys who led them rode ahead, drumming bare heels into donkeys' sides. A caique was unloading bright tiles on the shore: and five dejected horses waited for the consular party. It was the scene of a David Roberts' picture, still unchanged.

In these waters, not far from Myra, one of the early naval battles between Byzantium and the Arabs was fought. Even now the proximity of Arabia is felt; the greetings and ejaculations—*merhaba, salaam aleikum, yallah*—are more Arabic than elsewhere; the nomad feeling and the gay rough view of life are here. But well-kept orange gardens and houses quickly building, inside and beyond the dunes, are altering the land described by Fellows and Texier a century ago. A bus now comes from Kash to Myra, sometimes twice a week and sometimes once in two months, they told us; the post is carried on horse-back in eight hours; the main difficulty is to get to these places, as it was in Fellows' time.

In his day, a priest remained to look after the shrine of St. Nicholas in summer when his flock escaped from the mosquitoes to the mountains. Now, mosquitoes and Greeks have both been wiped away, and the remote village with its white-washed school and its growing prosperity is inhabited by two hundred Turks from Epirus. In spite of all, a Mediterranean softness is left, the Aegean blood is still about in the faces of the girls, and there is a sort of clemency among the gardens. But the church of St. Nicholas behind its cypress trees has lost what life it had, drowned to the height of its vaulting by the present level of the valley floor, and excavated in a pit filled with brambles.

The merchants of Bari in the 10th and 11th centuries were familiar with the Levant. Their city had in fact been held from A.D. 842 to 871 by an Arab sultan, who gave a passport for Cairo and Alexandria to a monk called Bernard, otherwise unknown, except that he travelled from Tarentum on a Saracen boat. By the end of the 10th century the Byzantine hold was firm again on Bari. Traders there would slip across to Constantinople in Venetian bottoms, so as to enjoy the Venetian facilities. In 1087, a Bari vessel making for Antioch with forty 'bourgeois and merchants', put in at Myra, and they decided to abduct the body of St. Nicholas on their return. They spoke about the project in Antioch to some Venetians, who remarked that they too had plans for the holy relic: it became a race between the Italians of the north and south, and the people of Bari won.

They found Myra in a state of disorder, just conquered for the caliph Harun by one of his generals, and the shrine deserted by all except three poor monks, who easily believed that their visitors came with authority to carry the relic away. The tomb was cracked open, and in it a marble urn half filled with oil was found, the bones jumbled and tampered with, and the head laid separate. All this the robbers took, and made a record sailing of eighteen days to Bari, where the holy oil was distributed to monasteries, and the bishop of Amiens, in 1100, travelled across the Alps to secure a phial. Celebrations and processions were organized; the relics, or what passed for such, spread and blossomed in churches throughout Europe; and the Normans built and endowed a cathedral for them, which still exists. On the feast of St. Nicholas, I was told some years ago, the saint's effigy is carried through the city of Bari, street by street, by devotees who feel the weight by the end of the day, and sometimes leave him for a while outside the taverns before carrying him on through the night. It makes a more cheerful life than the deserted thickets of Myra. As for the Venetians, who arrived too late, they were not to be outdone, and brought home a set of bones of their own, recognized as those of the uncle of the original saint and honoured together with St. Theodore.[1]

The flavour of commerce which hangs round these trans-actions has perhaps destroyed the atmosphere of holiness of the shrine; or perhaps mere emptiness has done it. The inter-esting but mildewed little basilica, built by Theo losius, and called by him Zion when Myra became the capital of Lycia, has no particular magic. Its former pillars lie fallen around it, and an arched apse 'renewed by the help of the Russians in 1852' is the only ornament, together with some poor frescoes and the ornate Isaurian sarcophagus which was pointed out as the tomb. D. B. thought the saint would have lain in the side chapel nearest the apse on the south, where orthodox holiness is more usually buried. There an obscure sarcophagus has a slab that looks as if it had been moved. The pieces of a balus-trade lie outside the narthex; and even their marble looks dull, in its well of bramble and fig and green shadows, and ruin. The meaning that once inhabited these forms has emigrated— to be carried from pub to pub in the concourse of the people in Bari; in Myra St. Nicholas is dead, buried in silt like the Byzantine city, and one walks away with relief to where the less holy deaths of the Lycians still speak from the high precipice where their tombs are carved.

'Moschus loves Philiota, the daughter of Demetrius', was found by Texier, scratched by some early shepherd with his knife.

Myra

We missed this, for we had short time to linger and it would take a week or so and a good deal of ability with cliffs to know the ins and outs of all the tombs of Myra. They cover the eastern and western faces of a height which Strabo mentions, on whose flat summit Byzantine and older patches of wall still show. Crowded on the rock face, with sculptured lobbies under porticoes, with inner excavated chambers and the familiar house façades of Lycia, the tombs recall a time that slips unobtrusively towards the Roman Empire and its theatre down below. The easy sculptured figures stand or sit, stripped for war or loosely gowned for banquets; the lions and bulls fight their oriental battle; and our French archaeologists were particularly stirred by the Artemis of Santorin or Thera, who stands on her double fish-tail between lion-heads, and holds her long locks with upraised arms under a high crown. Her mixed world was moving unaware to unexpected cataclysms. On the tomb that lingers in my mind a draped woman sits with two men standing to left and right of her. The first already shows the rigidity of the coming Byzantine drapery; the other stands naked in the classic past; he has a shaven head with a triple coil of hair upright upon it—the coil that Arab parents leave today when they shave their boys' heads with a Gillette blade, for the angel to lift them by into Paradise. The woman sits there, between a bare past and a shrouded future; and the boy lays his hand with tenderness on her shoulder, as if he too felt how all things were moving away from her for ever.

On the flat land, at the foot of the high cliff, the passing of time is shown more brutally by the silt of the gorges of Demre, which has covered the Byzantine with eighteen feet of soil and has left little of the more inland Roman town standing except ends of columns among *agnus castus* and roots of asphodel. The theatre remains,[2] fitted on higher ground into the rocky western necropolis. Its piers and arched vomitoria, and seats that overlap the semicircle in the Asiatic pattern, are all open to what must have been a view of the estuary before the sand-dunes came. There is a Roman petrified solidity about the theatre, in spite of the smooth mortarless beauty of its stone. The high podium—eight feet and an inch—belongs to a late time when the fashion of wild beasts had been brought from the West into the shows of Asia and Cicero was collecting panthers in his province, for Rome.

The capitals, the tragic masks and ornaments that Texier found here have mostly vanished; and the shepherd-boys of Myra, with nothing better to do all day, continue to deface the sculpture of the tombs. The government attends to all it can, but is faced by an almost insoluble problem in places where the antiquities are so scattered and so lonely. When I was in Ankara, I suggested that village schoolmasters might be made official guardians in their districts, with a very small increase of salary—and this would not only put the responsibility in the hands of someone on the spot, but would induce them, as they became interested, to train their pupils with more than their parents' respect for the history of their own past in their own land. I hope this suggestion may be adopted. At present, the ruins are safest in the nomad regions; and as settlement in houses increases, the ancient worked stone, 'as beautiful as marble', is doomed.

Only one of the inscriptions is Greek—on the tomb of Arsaces from Myndus in the north: the main impression of Myra is barbarian overlaid with Rome. Its importance grew under the Empire; it became, with Patara, the chief port of Lycia; and the theatre, which held about eleven thousand spectators, still expresses, alone in the harvested stubble, a crowded but provincial prosperity.

We left it for the half-hour's walk back to Demre, and found the village in midday leisure sitting at café tables under trees. The market was over; the sun lay full on the wide rural street and its gardens; the camels were heaving themselves up, free of their loads. They moved into the hills with bronze bells clanking between the saddle prongs. Empty black homespun sacks woven with white stripes, which had held the maize they had carried from inland valleys, were now tucked under ropes, with the scales they had brought to weigh them. The procession of heaving outlines moved easily above the fences, as if a small and mobile landscape had taken to imitating the slower-moving ridges of the dunes.

We too rode along a flat stretch westward, behind a promontory that separates Myra from Andriace, now Andraki, her ancient port. Whether she used it exclusively or had a river-harbour of her own as well, now buried, I cannot discover; but Andriace must have been the main harbour; it was wide enough for a ferry to obtain a monopoly to cross it,[3] and was a station for grain-ships that sailed to Italy from Egypt, avoiding the current of Crete. From its land-locked basin St. Paul, as a prisoner, saw the last of Asia—a shallow bay, surrounded by many ranges of the Lycian hills.

Hadrian built his granary here as at Patara—seven long store-rooms opening on a two-hundred-foot façade, with busts of himself and his empress on brackets under an inscription. A small double window is over each door, and that was all the light except for a few narrow openings like arrow slits in the outer walls. Whether these storehouses were meant for the grain of the country, or whether for grain in transit is not known; but they must have supplied the Roman armies on their way through to the Parthian, Persian or Armenian wars.

Scattered sarcophagi were on our path as we rode, drowning to their lids in marsh and sand; and after a while we had to leave our horses, and scramble by a dry hillside to where the granary stood, roofless, with its broken pediment a puzzle to architects, but otherwise intact. Its rooms were crowded with bay trees and bushes of myrtle: Mehmet calls them the plants of peace. The low range of hills stretched behind, cheerful with its own secret business, thick with vegetation to the edge of the marsh, and scented in the warmth of the afternoon.

Some caiques had pushed their way up the short estuary of the Andraki river, to a landing pier and a mill, where the corn trade, dwindled to this trickle, continues. Above the entrance of the bay a Hellenistic tower rose among the trees: and across the swamp and water of the ancient harbour an opposite ridge, uncultivated and overgrown like ours, was dotted with sarcophagi and ruins.

I was tired, and left the Hellenistic tower, and the river which D. B. rode to examine at its source. I sat in the sun, thinking of Hadrian and the security of Rome, when 'the cities all shone with brightness and grace, and all the earth was adorned as a garden . . . The smoke and the beacons of friends and of foes have vanished from the plains, as if the wind had blown them beyond land and sea. Instead have entered every grace of spectacle and a countless multitude of games. So that like a holy unquenchable fire holiday never ceases, but moves around, now here, now there, but somewhere always'.[4]

Beyond the loading of the caiques, far beyond the horizon, the Empire lay, a lake with scarce a ripple; and the few waves that crashed at the frontier edges were rarely heard or seen. It was a law-encircled sea. The swamps puckered over it slowly, and the centuries clogged it, like the harbour I was looking at, below.

A flock was trickling down the hillside, in scattered groups like drops towards the stream. It is always the image of the *flock* in the New Testament: no external compulsion holds it, and the partnership of the faithful is never a unity constrained in walls. The closed door is the image used for exclusion or death.

The flock is nothing but a heartfelt direction. It moves to its desire until the unity that guided it is lost or forgotten, and then it falls to pieces too: and locks and walls and the uses of constraint are remembered, administration rules instead of serving, and the closed door becomes an emblem of order: and this not only in the Roman world. But the Greeks, perhaps because of their doubts, kept the free unity—the feeling of a flock that seeks and belongs to the same pastures; and the pattern of their civilization, in the 4th century and after, came to be a badge no longer of blood but of mind, Hellenic in essence, but not dependent on climate or race. This conquered in the wake of Alexander, and spread through Asia, and tamed the victories of Rome.

Therefore, in spite of order we lament the Roman victories, although in the West we should be exiles without them. For we know that the flock is happiest with its own shepherds; and no external fold, however safe, should hold it long.

We rode back to *Elfin* in the evening and bathed in the sunset water. The dunes were caught in a flood of fire and the pebbles on the sea-floor kept their brightness and shone through the green water with little facets of light. As the *Elfin* set out through the twilight, a grey crane and a solitary man squatting to wash before his prayer were alone on the vast semicircle of the sands. By some illusion, the delta land between the dunes and the crack of the Myra gorge looked as if it lay below sea-level as we sailed along it. Where the sands end, and a cape comes down, a shallow runnel lets sea-fish into a *dalyan* or lake, beneath whose waters old buildings are seen by fishermen, and at whose northern point Fellows found two ancient towers, with a city on the ridge five thousand feet above. The evening was closing down and we saw little, except mists and high mountains above them and, low behind us, the blue promontories of the western hills. In the dusk, we turned the cape, and saw the lights of Phineka, now Finike, at the bottom of their bay, and the level wall of the Anatolian plateau behind them.

15

THE CHELIDONIAN CAPE

Magic

Aegean sea,
Where three boats out of thirty may escape from wreck.
MENANDER, The Flute Girl.

From the mountains of the Solymi; even thence he saw Odysseus as he sailed
over the deep. ODYSSEY V, 282.

A MAIN STREET AND A FEW SIDE LANES, A SMALL HOTEL and a clean *lokanta* have blossomed in Finike from the three houses of Fellows' and Texier's day. We left our French friends there in a lane where an old-fashioned carriage was waiting, round and long as a segment of sausage, of which the lower half, inside, was padded, the upper decorated with sequins, mirrors, and small windows at the level of a reclining eye. Its horse stood with his head in the shade and a patient look, as of something that has already turned out of life into history, while the sun moved round his quarters. A few motor-cars and lorries, old but not as old as the carriage, came and went lurching over holes. The road, after break-neck adventures from Xanthus southward, makes from Finike with good engineering up the ancient Arycanda (Alağir Chay) valley, to Elmali and the levels of the plateau; and the atmo-sphere of Finike was that of an infinite leisure dropping as if without a thoroughfare into the harbour.

This was in 1952. But the place is growing. A coast-road, two years later, had already reached the cliff which Alexander and his bodyguard were obliged to circumvent by water, and will affect all this district: even on our first visit, the nomads

157

were beginning to build new houses round the marshes of the Limyra water, where little ancient cities lie buried whose names are scarcely known. On the rising ground, Limyra remains—a hillside of tombs, a Roman theatre, Byzantine walls—and a fortress, which we left unexplored on its height. Gaius Caesar[1] died there on his way to Italy.

Where the plain begins, the water gushes out in the sudden manner of the limestone, with a carved sarcophagus beside it, in clear coiling green streams round a mill. The ancient main road ran there, fit only now for a jeep that can ford the river, which has wandered far away from the Roman bridge that spanned it. The houses thin out long before reaching it, and when we left the last village we found the nomads around us, with tents newly pitched after their summer pastures in the hills.

There seems to be a fitness in the relationship between them and the graves round which their camps so often sit—even beyond the natural explanation of water, which persists while habitations come and go. Here in Limyra, tombs crowded each other so that the curve of the hill was built up out of their tiers, like a convex theatre that looks on the outer world instead of inwards towards its human actors: and the tents and the huts of rushes scattered among the tombs resembled them in all except a greater fragility, while the flowering scilla, *urginea maritima*, lifted its pale panicles as if it could blossom equally among the living or the dead.

The life of insecurity is the nomad's achievement. He does not try, like our building world, to believe in a stability which is non-existent; and in his constant movement with the seasons, in the lightness of his hold, puts something right, about which we are constantly wrong. His is in fact the reality, to which the most solid of our structures are illusion; and the ramshackle tents in their crooked gaiety, with cooking-pots propped up before them and animals about, show what a current flows round all the stone erections of the ages. The finest ruin need only be lamented with moderation, since its living essence long ago entered the common stream. No thought of this kind is likely to come into the head of the Turkish Yürük (though it could be familiar to the imagination of the Arab); they are happy to shelter their goats in the warmth or the shade that they find, whether the ruins be of Nineveh or Rome. In Limyra they were partly settled and partly arriving from the mountains, with long trains of camels and flocks, and horses straying loosely on the wandering track. Their women invited us, where the tents and pillows were stacked in order; they were cheerful and fierce, unlike the peasant, and dressed in brighter colours—equals of their men or of anyone, as one may be if one lives under the hardness of necessity and makes insecurity one's refuge.

We too, on our sea way, were about to hazard ourselves on a small scale, for we were going to double the Chelidonian Cape, where one's safety depends on northerly weather, and who can tell how that will last from one day to the next? On the far side was the Chimaera, in her enchanted land: we were leaving the matter-of-fact world.

We were not for underestimating magic—a life-conductor like the sap between the tree-stem and the bark. We know that it keeps dullness out of religion and poetry. It is probable that without it we might die.

Everything in the nature of inspiration belongs to it; and there will be a gloomy world when prophets, artists, and tactful women think they can do without it. The politician and the business man could give it a few moments in their day. For it is easily attainable. It requires a mere suspension of activity—so that the self, in a passive air, may become pure reception, while mystery flowers into an articulate mood with as little interference as possible from the human channel it uses.

The Chelidonian Cape

This is magic, within reach of us all; a flash where the universe surges up through a creature, who becomes ear, or eye—an unresisting vehicle—void of self, filled and replenished with sights and sounds and feelings that move in and out of perception, so that in his small concreteness, according to his capacity and abnegation, the roots of being may grow. This is what the egocentric loses, and substitutes for it his miserable person. And perhaps magic alone is the cause of the happiness of primitive, and true country people, for whom all pleasures of sophistication are compensated, if they only knew it, by this awareness.

There are not so many places left where it reigns without interruption, and of all those I know, the coast of Lycia was most magical: especially on this, the first of *Elfin*'s southern voyages, when all of us—D. B., Mehmet and I—all except Hüseyin—were new to it; and Hüseyin himself enhanced our legendary feelings by his obvious anxiety as we neared the Chelidonian cape.

Beyond lies the huge Pamphylian bay; and beyond that again, rarely seen from so far, the semicircle of the Cilician Taurus; and all that coast until you reach Antalya, said Hüseyin, is defenceless against the south wind if it blows.

And one must remember how small the *Elfin* was, and, for all her purring engines, a slow little goer along those beetling shores. "We must be sure," said D. B.—looking at me fiercely as if I were the one who liked bad weather—"of three fine days"; and then one might possibly explore the exposed little anchorages and turn back before Antalya, while the good breeze held.

I kept myself well in hand, not to show too much enthusiasm over the uninhabited country, which was liable to trouble a consular conscience. Luckily a chrome mine exists in that roadless district: I ignored the Chimaera, and talked of chrome.

It was afternoon when we left, and the *embat*, or afternoon wind, was against us: it rises from the day's heat like an exhalation, and blows against the land in any direction on these indented coasts.

The fifteen miles of the bay took us two hours. Finike sank to a line of poplars against Ak Dag and the high level background of the plateau; the few fields and long woodlands of the cape grew clear as we approached. Somewhere at the foot of their slopes was Gagae, one of the Lycian towns, but we could not find it. We saw only a miniature overgrown castle-ruin, with steps to a tiny cove. The *embat* died as we neared the great cape, the south-west point of Asia Minor. A smooth unbroken swell was on the farther side, as if the sea were swaying from its roots on its own shadows, all of one piece and gently, like a weed.

From these mountains of the Solymi—the Tahtali or Timber-mountains of the Turks—Poseidon looked out and saw Odysseus when he left Calypso's island. The summit however, the beautiful pyramid of Solyma 7,800 feet high, where in the snow, the legends say, the roses blossom, and groans are heard to summon the Muslims to Paradise,[2] is not visible from the cape. Wave after wave of rising hills approach it, and stretch blue arabesques above the sea, and rise to near four thousand feet within four miles or so of the cape. The cape itself, wooded on the west to its small lighthouse, faces south and east, with sharp cliffs ranked in deep water like Homeric shields. The coast, as the Mediterranean pilot puts it, is 'steep-to'. And its five islets, dry and empty, are a home for eagles, and a resting-place for swallows in their migrations.

This was the boundary imposed on Asia by the Roman Republic when Antiochus the Great, after the battle of Magnesia, agreed to remain south of Taurus and the Chelidonian islands. In the recess of the great bay, the last round with Hannibal was fought. He commanded the left wing of Antiochus' navy—triremes with three seven-banked and four six-banked galleys among them, for Alexander's successors were the builders of the largest ships in the ancient world. The fleet, thirty-seven ships in all, rowed from Cilicia in a straight line of battle.

The Rhodian sailors on the Roman side were hugging the shore in column, when the navies met. They had to form their line while already five of their number and Eudamus their admiral were engaged. Here the excellence of their seamanship was shown, for they had drawn in too close to the land to deploy, and yet managed without panic—each galley as it came up pushing ahead into the enemy crowd to leave a free space for its neighbour—till the whole fleet was in, and Eudamus rescued, who had almost been surrounded.

Hannibal and the ships which followed him began to retire; nor could the Rhodians pursue, since many of their rowers were sick and therefore exhausted; and while they were eating and resting in the open water, Eudamus saw the enemy towing home their lame and crippled ships with hawsers from open vessels, hardly more than twenty of them moving off undamaged. 'From the bridge of the flagship he called for silence and exclaimed: "Stand up and look upon a glorious sight." Every man stood up, and seeing the confusion and panic of the enemy, cried almost with one voice "Let us pursue" . . . But when Hannibal was close to land, fearing that they might be detained by the wind near a hostile coast, they returned . . . and with difficulty towed to Phaselis the captured seven-banked ship, which had been struck by one blow from a much smaller Rhodian at the first onset.'

This battle kept Hannibal from Lycia, and let the Rhodians hold the narrow sea of Patara as we noticed when we passed: and one may say that the Chelidonian cape in general was the boundary between the Greek and the Phoenician seas. Greek galleys coming from the north must often have passed, with oars and sail and a certain trepidation, and, like Hüseyin, thought of the cape as a curtain that opened on wonders and dangers unknown.   Cimon was here in the early days just after the Persian wars, rowing from Cnidus with two hundred galleys built wide in the deck for soldiers.   He laid siege to Phaselis, which held by the Persians and repulsed him till the Chians made peace between them;[3] and he then sailed on to the Eurymedon.   Pericles soon after, doubling the cape with fifty galleys, found not one Persian vessel beyond the Chelidonian isles.[4]   Melesander came here in 430 B.C., to collect tribute and keep the trade route open from Phaselis and Phoenicia, and, going up the country into Lycia with a force of Athenians from the ships and the allies, was killed.[5]   Alcibiades, and the disgusted Spartans, came from Miletus in the time of Tissaphernes; and, in 401 B.C., Samius the Spartan admiral, coasted down to help Cyrus and his Ten Thousand on the Cilician coast.[6]

As we moved between the headland and the islands, we saw a caique hurrying with a furtive look towards the open horizon of the east.   "A Greek," said Hüseyin, "she has been sheltering so as to reach Turkish water by nightfall, and will fish almost in sight of Antalya, and rely on her strong engines to escape."   She grew small in the afternoon light that lay in patches, like discarded armour on the surface of the sea.

We turned northward, and watched clouds piling windless towers on Solyma as we kept near the inhospitable shore.   The swell, scarcely stirring, felt as if with fingers along its shallow caves.   The cliffs, almost vertical from their unseen floor, grew trees in rocky fissures; one could see the difference of two vegetations where the limestone was knotted in strong tangles with the jumbled landscape of the chrome.   Veins of that strange metal zigzagged in silver bands through the faces of the cliffs shorn away in their long battle with the south.   We felt no more than a truce in the deceptive calm of land and sea, as if *Elfin* were venturing between two hosts who watched her, leaning on their spears.   There were no houses on the land, till the bay of Ardatchan opened, and showed at its far end some cultivated fields; then we nosed on again under high walls in the twilight, looking for a safe opening in the rocks; and suddenly, as Hüseyin turned in darkness, felt the silkiness of quiet water. We were in a little cove called Porto Genovese, often taken as a refuge on this fierce coast.

Even here the wind could reach us. It pounced down the hill behind us to the sea; and I heard Hüseyin, as I lay awake, tightening and altering the anchor, while *Elfin* fidgeted in jerks, as if stung by flies.

In the morning, we found ourselves in the small circular cove where Beaufort saw deer browsing among the bushes. We found only some late ruins half swallowed in trees, and a small beach like a sickle. The north wind held, and we went on, round the defences of Mt. Phoenix, whose clefts and precipices throw their shadows over the Lycian city of Olympus.

The coast beyond opens to a long stretch of sand and flat-topped pines, and no villages are in sight. Smoke from nomad tents rises among the trees. In the wooded hills is the Chimaera. But the town of Olympus, when it lived, was in a rocky defile where the sand meets the mountain and a clear perennial stream comes down, and curves round the piers of a ruined bridge by an ancient quay, under two little fortresses, Genoese and Byzantine, out to sea, through a bank of gravel.

The Genoese castle must have given its name to our anchorage, and, on the opposite bank of the river, on a small height of its own, is the other—a Byzantine castle built with small stones and fragments of marble pushed in here and there, all in ruin. A way runs beneath it to an old High Street, along what must once have been a river-harbour which the mountain background closes. On the south of the river too there are walls and arches and sarcophagi, so lost in thickets that we could not push in among them, but peered at them as we rowed the *Elfin*'s dinghy, lifted over the shallow embankment of the sea.

Olympus

Olympus was described by Cicero as an ancient city full of riches and works of art, and its records go back to the 2nd century B.C., when it issued coins and soon after belonged to the Lycian federation. But all that one sees now is later. Its defiles festoon it with Gothic shadows pushed deep into the mountain cloisters, where pirates held out in the early years of Rome.

In 79 B.C., Publius Servilius Vatia came with the young Julius Caesar in his train, when a robber called Zenicetes held the towns and fortified himself in the recesses of Phoenix. A victory at sea made it possible to capture Olympus, and the robber set fire to his own house and perished.[7]

Prosperity must have returned. Tombs of late Christian patterns crowd each other on the flat land, below older ones on the hill by the city wall. The riverside, where the citizens walked up and down a paved quay in the cool of the evening, shows scraps of mosaic floor or Byzantine lintels, church doors under rounded arches, the graceful transition between the ancient and medieval worlds. Hidden in thick trees, the temple door carved for Marcus Aurelius lives on. We saw it gleaming from the slope of the hill as we scrambled among tombs: they had attracted us by their shape, which we had not seen before —barrel-vaulted masonry and stucco, closed by small square slabs of stone running in grooves, often inscribed with late Greek letters. From their height, where they climbed at the fork of the valley, we looked down and saw the marble of the temple door, between the path and a swamp beyond: and took another hour to find it, hidden so deep in a dampness of trees. It rose fifteen feet high, its square, egg-and-dart cornices cleanly cut, with that feeling for perfection by which the classic keeps man triumphant through all his ruin. The fine Roman lettering of the inscription lay heaped among the roots beside it.

In the shadows, the walls of a later palace too survived.

The Chelidonian Cape

Surrounded by its canyons, hidden among its forests, Olympus lies like a mosaic of the ages on the valley floor. It looked to me as if—apart from those robber interludes—it had slipped quietly from its Lycian to its Byzantine years. Then the preoccupation with defence began—no doubt against the Arabs—and the comfortable Byzantine windows were blocked to make functional walls; and after that the rough Crusader work intruded on the High Street and its past. The Genoese town, we thought, lay walled below its castle, among laurel trees south of the stream, with a round tower and a connecting bridge now lost—all too deeply overgrown to be explored. Nothing was certain to our casual wandering except the lingering uneasiness of a late age, when rapine—no longer a sport for young men who go seafaring in galleys—had become the keynote of life. This was the 'Gothic' quality of Olympus, threatening and medieval. It had overlaid the classic ease there may have been, where, amid murders and exile, the kindness of civilization was still a remembered pattern; the ancient recumbent lion with his long gaze of memory and contemplation had stood up, as it were, and become rampant in the medieval coat of arms.

Two years later, we again visited Olympus. The flowering oleanders hung over the river and filled the valley from side to side. The nomads were about, and herds of goats went eating their way among the torrent boulders; the young black bulls came roaring up the Byzantine High Street by the stream. Its water ran brown and still, between edges of watercress and frogs; and the precipices of Phoenix suspended their naked skeletons above the valley. But a miracle had happened: the sunlight had rubbed away their sharpness and wrapped them in azure, as if the magic of life, the invisible air, an intangible weaving, were more enduring than all the deaths it has to encounter and overcome.

CHIMAERA TO PHASELIS

The Pool of Time

Godhead itself is seen
In flash of an ecstatic hand that holds
High in the wind the whirling tambourine.   EURIPIDES, Bacchae.

Chimaera the unconquerable . . . of divine birth was she and not of men, in
front a lion, and behind a serpent, and the midst a goat; and she breathed dread
fierceness of blazing fire.   ILIAD, VI. 180.

THE LYCIAN COINS FOUND BY FELLOWS ON HIS TRAVELS
bore the images of Bellerophon, Pegasus, the Sphinx, or
Pan, as well as the later figure of Apollo; and Bellerophon
—although he came from Corinth and Argos—belongs particularly to Lycia. Here he landed, as a handsome young man,
ignorant that the letter he carried to the King signified his
death; was sent through the defiles to meet Chimaera; and,
mounted on Pegasus, slew her from the air with arrows.
And Pegasus, born near the sources of Ocean, the child of
Medusa and Poseidon, who carried the thunder of Zeus and
was thought by some to be the horse of Aurora, can be seen

any fine day after rain, with white wings and billowy quarters
and misty hooves tangled in cirrus clouds, that rise from the
Chelidonian bay and float round the pyramid of Solyma above
the range of Phoenix. Chimaera too continues to glimmer
from her woods across the sea with an unchanging fire, visible
to sailors until the arrows of the sun extinguish her in daylight.
She is little over an hour's ride inland from the long beach
north of Olympus; and we determined to call at the chrome
mine round the headland of the bay, to find horses (without
wings) and ride up to her.

The mine owns a wooden jetty and five or six houses in a
small bay. It has three hundred workmen who were tun-
nelling in hills out of sight, and the young owner and his wife,
who received us charmingly on our second visit, were absent
too: they had gone, four or five hours by motor-launch from
the then roadless coast, to Antalya.

Their manager came out with surprised politeness and,
having heard our request, sent horses round the southern
promontory to where the shore extended under flat-topped
pines—the nearest point between Chimaera and the sea.

No houses showed in this landscape. The uncultivated hills
surrounded us with roots of pines like those painted by the
Chinese. They made a twisted yellow and black background to a small delta, where mares and foals of the nomads
browsed. Hot, resinous scents were all about it, and our
ponies picked their way among boulders; they trembled with
excitement that made them stumble whenever a mare with
long, free-flowing mane and her little one behind her trotted
sedately by. It was good to be riding again. The pommelled
crusader saddle had stirrups beaten out of a sheet of metal, to
protect the foot against sharp rocky corners. One buckles
them long, and holds the leg straight, as if standing, as they did
when the butt-end of a lance rested upon the toe.

The path soon began to climb; the maquis closed about it,

with blossoming heath pink and white, and myrtle buds
sprayed like pearls along their boughs; even the burnet was
starred over its surly cushions with festoons of small six-
petalled creamy flowers. After one and a quarter hours of
easy climbing, we reached a shallow dell where grey limestone
cropped up through the rusty schists of the chrome; and here
the Chimaera, small and very sooty, like a hearth, poured a
tired flame out of the hillside, beside—or inside—a temple to
Hephaestus, whose shapeless fragments pushed through the
grass above it here and there.

Seneca and Pliny describe it, and it was put in the wrong
district by Strabo, and Captain Beaufort, in 1818, reported it as
a brilliant and perpetual fire which no water could quench,
and which would not roast stolen meat. In the small Byzantine church of which an apse and two windows stand in an
enclosure nearby, he found an inscription to 'Theodulos, the
servant of God'.[1]

Any number of other inscriptions must lie about here, some
of them in half-buried fragments on the ground: one of them,
on a pedestal, is dedicated to the Emperor Hadrian by the town
council of Olympus, and a piece of another is built into the
rough wall above Chimaera. Her fierce days are over.
Wedged in between the ruined Hephaestion and the painted
apse of the chapel, she burns domestic and dull between the
dogmas, like many a housewife before and after, with only that
meagre flame to show how long a journey of primeval fire
still feeds her in spite of all. One must look at her from the
sea to know her power: there, when on our return we left the
Pamphylian shore, we saw her beckoning, a witch-light in
the darkness of the hills.

As we rode down again from the scrub, to the evening fresh-
ness of the river that travels underground beneath the pines,
the nomads talked about their pendulum life, their seven
lowland months and five months in the hills. They warded

off mares who came trotting, with tails flowing like Greek draperies behind them, lifting heads and opening nostrils with feminine whinnies of welcome. I wondered, as I have so often done in Arabia, at the *aristocracy* of them all—that lean and vital quality shared by the nomad creatures—the thin Saluki dogs, the horses and goats hungry and free, the shepherd-girl's little triangular face and Mona Lisa lips, the wide-awake eyes of the lads and easy equal manners, meeting their life as it comes—the loveliness of even the old women at the well.

It is easy for the peasant, and for all of us who live in civilization and think to make the world more habitable, to point out that the nomad does very little. He leaves things as he finds them, destroying them in a small way if it suits him. He does not spend his life as we do in altering the accidents that happen to us so as to make them more bearable—but he accepts them with gaiety and endures them with fortitude, and this is his triumph and his charm. We may think reasonably enough that we dominate circumstances more than he does, since we adapt them to our needs: but he has discovered that the meaning of life is more important than its circumstance—and this freedom of the soul, in which all things that happen come and go, makes him splendid—him and his gaunt women and dogs and horses, on the edge of starvation in the rain and the sun.

His life does not allow him to forget the greater size of the world; and no amount of civilization is worth the loss of this fundamental sense of proportion between the universe and man.

Perhaps, I thought as I rode along, this is the very point where the Greek path, after the 5th century, began to turn downhill.

The Greeks too accepted a world greater than themselves in the early Ionian days and the centuries that followed; its walls were out of sight and they made willingly towards them.

Only when knowledge could detect, or feel that it detected, a boundary, did the pressure of the cage begin to close. Then happiness was at an end, until the horizon could be widened once more to lead beyond human knowledge, for the nomad dies in prison, and so does a man, in a world that he feels too small.

Zeno, a tall young merchant, came from Phoenician Cyprus with his bales of purple. In a bookshop in Athens he picked up Xenophon's memories of Socrates, and asked the bookseller where such men could still be found; and the bookseller, seeing Crates, who was passing at that moment, told the stranger to follow him. He became a student, and founded the Stoic School:[2] and perhaps, in that scarcely perceptible moment which divides the right-hand from the left-hand choice at its beginning, something then happened in our world. For the people who had discovered and been hurt by the bars of their cage turned gratefully to the Asiatic renunciation, and forgot the Aegean zest for living while they searched for a new horizon in the minds of men.

The Stoic ages that followed have never completely left us. They turned from the external universe and questioned the human soul inwardly, for such contentment as it requires, and did what they could to loosen its mortal attachments. And it is ever a twilight world that abstains or refuses. The Ionian dawn was lost, and the bars of the cage pressed in; until a later teaching surmounted the barrier, and stretched the world out again into its unfenced frame. Happiness, as I rode down towards the beach in the evening, seemed to me to belong to those three ages, ever with a growing awareness: to the nomad, whose infinity lies about him unquestioned; to the Aegean sailing without fear towards a yet undiscovered horizon; and to those, in the religions of our time, 'whose service is perfect freedom' since they have seen their bars melted and infinity renewed. Freedom is the secret. They can accept the cage of this world because it does not really exist, and they live in their liberty beyond it—with a delight different in its accent from the Stoic's endurance.

So it seemed to me, who am no theologian, but must decide, like any other human being, on what is good for my own soul. And it pleased me, while the boy Omer walked by the pony's head and held its bridle in narrow places, to think of him and myself enjoying the same liberty in two worlds different in degree but not in kind.

That night we anchored by the jetty of the chrome mine, and started northward before the dawn; and I was awakened by D. B.'s voice, calling down to me from the deck.

"You may never see this again," said he, as I emerged: and there, on the horizon's arc, far and small, but sharp and black, beneath the sun that opened like a yellow rose, and beyond invisible Cilician beaches, was the outline of the Taurus.

On our left, where the coast ran out in a flat-topped snout, we were making for Phaselis, the modern Tekrova. We were only an hour and a half north of the chrome mine at *Elfin's* pace.

Phaselis, according to Cicero, was a Greek town inhabited by Lycians; the two had evidently become indistinguishable in his day. It was obliged to keep on friendly terms with the pirates, who often touched there, and Livy describes it as the first land sighted by travellers from Rhodes to Cilicia. The Rhodians chose it as their base against Antiochus and Hannibal because it gave them a long view of any fleet approaching from east or south. But even then it must have been declining, with marshes encroaching around it, for Livy goes on to describe the unhealthiness of the summer climate, and the unaccustomed odour which spread disease among the Rhodian rowers; and Pompey, who visited it on his flight, found it a small and shrunken town.

Cicero seems to have been wrong in calling it Lycian; the typical Lycian tomb is absent along all this coast, and Phaselis

was Greek in very early days, bought—it was said—by Lakios
from a shepherd and paid for with salt fish. An Argive or
Rhodian colony, it belonged in the 6th century B.C. to the
settlers of Naucratis in Egypt, and must have been usefully
placed for sailors on a northern voyage.   After holding for the
Persians and resisting Cimon, it joined the Athenian League,
and was important enough for six ships to be sent from Athens
in the early years of the Peloponnesian war, to protect the
passage of its trade.   In Murray's *Handbook* it is said to have
been famous for its attar of roses.   And it was hither that the
envoys who had met him brought Alexander, on his way into
Pamphylia.   So much and more one may gather from books:
but who can weave, to repeat it, the spell of Phaselis in her
solitude in the dawn?

In the Republic, Er, a Pamphylian, saw, in the midst of
light, the ends of the chains of heaven let down from above:
and perhaps he remembered this coast, on the edge of his
lands.   The mild cone of Solyma rises from it on even slopes,
which the evening and morning kindle from west or east of
the Pamphylian bay. Ravines curve like wings from the
clear summit, with feathered ridges darkened by their trees;
and the whole realm settles gently, in smooth decreasing gra-
dients to the sea.

There, in the most southerly of Phaselis' three harbours we
anchored, in a small waveless bay, under whose surface ran
the trace of an ancient mole.   Seven pedestals of marble had
been thrown on their faces in the water, to make a landing
stage on to a level isthmus.   The pines bent towards each other,
beside a flat acropolis, on a low but sheer peninsula above.
A double wall appeared there—roofed with stone slabs, three
feet or more across, and hollow but for cross-stones here and
there inside it.   Most of it had fallen away, eaten and under-
mined by the sea; and the whole town on top, and the way up
to it, were clustered with bay trees and thorns so thick that

little of the ruins could be distinguished, except vaults broken down and mortar, which showed the lateness of the building. From the south, when we sailed round, we saw the cliffs fallen away with their walls and outer houses, and many pear-shaped cavities cut in two by the ruin of the earth, and lined with stucco—evidently store-places for grain.

On the north, shuffled by earthquakes and strangled in branches, the acropolis wall still showed the fine-cut blocks of its prime if one clambered among them; but it was on the isthmus, below, that one could fancy the city yet breathing, though in dreams only—entranced like the sleeping beauty, blanketed in time and forgetfulness, and overgrown with thorns.

The earth here, on level ground, was less encumbered, and a stone or marble thoroughfare led almost clear through the glade. Four steps rose along either side to palaces that had been rebuilt or had fallen in later epochs. Fellows mentions a stadium, but he and Beaufort place it farther north, and the fact that our space was paved, with drains let in across it, and that it led from one harbour to the other and sloped towards the sea, made us think it a street—though we could see no trace of stadium, or of theatre either, farther on. The finest buildings faced this thoroughfare; a temple, with Trajan's name and oak and ivy leaves carved on its cornices, lay tumbled in chaos across it; and arches of stone, massive Roman sub-structures, stood beyond.

Where the isthmus slopes down again, pine trees hang over the middle harbour, enclosing the minute clear proportions of its piers and quays. Traces of a small temple are on this headland under the pines; and beyond it, following the coast northward, the third harbour opens in what is now a swamp that trickles to the sea. The hill beyond was the city necropolis, whose tombs lie scattered among forest shadows— sarcophagi, or barrel vaults with square stone openings and sliding doors. On the shore, partly fallen, with doorposts standing amid a heap of ruined columns, are two mausoleums or perhaps little private temples for the dead. They are slipping into the sea that eats them slowly. One sarcophagus lies lidless in the waves; and another, with lion-snout of marble and a headless, toga'd figure, is slanting on its way.

The Roman aqueduct strides inland across the neck of the swamp from the north, where the water probably came tunnelled from the ground. Nine or ten yellow arches of polygonal stones, with a grey stone cornice above them, show through the pine-tree tops. An inferior later work of rubble and mortar was added—for the city continued to be inhabited into Christian times, and had bishops before it died—and a circular cistern now heaped in earth once housed the aqueduct water. Near it, beyond the north-west corner of the great street, we came by accident on seven broken shafts of temple columns, sunk and almost hidden—a temple in antis with eight-pillared peristyle—perhaps the one dedicated to Athena, where Achilles' spear was kept.[3]

The hours went by and even the south wind was forgotten. A strange feeling held us, as if we were not looking at the landscape about us, but down, through layer upon layer of limpid water, into the past transparencies of time. In my childhood, I have lain so for hours, peering from a boulder into the pool of a Dartmoor stream, which the current had missed. There its life went on, in a filtered light, a subtle brilliant obscurity, surrounded by stillness like a mirror—close but unapproachable, so that the roots or the stones I leaned on became divided into two separated selves, by the thin elemental line of water—the present and the past, and yet the same.

Such are Time and the things that move about in it when the living current with its streaks of quicksilver has left them; and such was Phaselis, solitary and almost forgotten in its pool.

Chimaera to Phaselis

The brightness of the Aegean filled its three harbours, and the current once ran here; and the stream of all our world poured briefly through with the troops of Alexander. What brought him to so remote a province, and kept him among its hills while the armies of Darius were strengthening in the East? A few stray words are all the help we have—the talk with Parmenio at Miletus, the disbanding of the navy, the omen of the eagle that foretold a conquest of the sea-ways from the shore.[4] It is the gleam of a fin, a movement among brown shadows in the pool; but the long thoughts that preceded the decisions, the influences of envoys and their persuasions, their very existences, have sunk indistinguishable into the settled dark.

When we visited Phaselis again another year, we discovered that the hamlet of Tekrova is just in sight behind it; the wood-cutters had been among the ruins; and the enchantment was broken. But we had seen it haunted. For one day, with the evening and the morning that followed, the shadows of the pines ran freely through the street and in the rooms of the ruined houses; the temple columns were as warm to the darting lizards as ever they had been to the hands of the devout who leaned against them; and amid the solitary rustlings—the breaking of a twig, a breath in the grasses, a ripple suddenly splashing on the sand—one could hear the voices of the dead city with their gaiety insubstantial and diminished, fading, elusive, like Eurydice, into the arms of night.

This was the farthest point of our voyage, and we left Antalya and the adventure of Alexander—yet with the hope of a return.

Hüseyin was getting restive, for we had been four days already, tempting the weather. We now sailed back, still with the north wind blowing, in the dark, past the Chelidonian cape to Finike. Thence we drove overland up the Alağir Chay past Arycanda, across cedar and juniper woods of the highlands, and skirted the gorges of Xanthus and left on one side the promontories of Caria; till we returned to the gentle outlines of Ionia, and saw the harbour of Smyrna and the modern city shining with lights in the evening, at the bottom of its bay.

DATES

FOR THE 5TH AND 4TH CENTURIES B.C.

(Reference in brackets to the chapters in which the event is mentioned)

490	Battle of Marathon (4).
485	Gelon Tyrant in Sicily (7).
480	Xerxes' Invasion of Greece: Thermopylae and Salamis (6)
c. 480	Birth of Euripides.
479	Battles of Plataea and Mycale.
478	Formation of the Confederacy of Delos (6).
c. 470	Birth of Socrates.
467 or 466	Cimon's victory on the Eurymedon (15).
c. 460	Birth of Hippocrates (6).
457	Building of the Long Walls at Athens (9).
455	First production by Euripides.
455–4	Defeat of the Athenian expedition against the Persians in Egypt (13).
454	Treasury of the Delos Confederacy removed to Athens (6).
450	Death of Cimon
449	Peace of Callias with Persia (7 and 9).
447	Parthenon begun.
446	Birth of Aristophanes.
c. 444	Birth of Xenophon.
442–1	Sophocles' *Antigone*.
441	Revolt of Samos from Athens. First Greek use of siege engines (3).
439	Surrender of Samos (3).
431	Peloponnesian War begins.
429	Death of Pericles.
427	Spartan admiral Alcidas urged to organize the revolt of Ionia. Butchers his prisoners at Myonnesus (3 and 7).
427	Fall of Mitylene.
424	Athens forces Chios to demolish her walls (2).

Dates

<table>
<tr><td>416</td><td>Capitulation and destruction of Melos (2).</td></tr>
<tr><td>415</td><td>Troades of Euripides.</td></tr>
<tr><td>414–3</td><td>Athenian siege and defeat at Syracuse (2 and 3).</td></tr>
<tr><td>412</td><td>Chian-Persian embassy to Sparta and revolt of Athenian subject-allies (2 and 3).</td></tr>
<tr><td>412</td><td>Samos becomes Athenian base (2 and 3).</td></tr>
<tr><td>412</td><td>Athenian siege of Chios. Revolt of Cnidus (7). Persian fleet at Aspendus (11). Athenian defeat off Syme (9). Treaties and negotiations with Tissaphernes (6 and 8).</td></tr>
<tr><td>411</td><td>Lysistrata of Aristophanes (13).</td></tr>
<tr><td>411</td><td>Oligarchy in Athens. Democracy in Samos. Athenian naval victories at Cynossema and Abydos. Pharnabazus' help to Spartans (3 and 7).</td></tr>
<tr><td>410</td><td>Democracy restored in Athens and Spartan peace offer refused (2).</td></tr>
<tr><td>408</td><td>Athens regains Byzantium.</td></tr>
<tr><td>408–7</td><td>Cyrus supersedes Tissaphernes as governor-general of western Asia Minor. Persia supports Sparta (7).</td></tr>
<tr><td>407</td><td>Alcibiades reinstated as Athenian general (2 and 3).</td></tr>
<tr><td>406</td><td>His defeat at Notium and withdrawal (2). Succeeded by Conon. Athenian victory at Arginusae and trial of the generals. Second Spartan peace offer refused (2).</td></tr>
<tr><td>406</td><td>Death of Euripides in Macedon. Death of Sophocles.</td></tr>
<tr><td>405</td><td>Grant of Athenian citizenship to Samos (3).</td></tr>
<tr><td>405</td><td>Athenian defeat at Aegospotami (2, 5 and 7).</td></tr>
<tr><td>405–4</td><td>Siege of Athens. Destruction of the Long Walls (3). Lysander establishes oligarchies. Dionysius dictator at Syracuse (13).</td></tr>
<tr><td>404</td><td>Tissaphernes at Miletus (7). Death of Alcibiades (7).</td></tr>
<tr><td>410–400</td><td>Date of the Lycian stele at Xanthus (12).</td></tr>
<tr><td>401</td><td>Cyrus and the Ten Thousand. Battle of Cunaxa (7). Tissaphernes reinstated in the maritime provinces of Asia Minor.</td></tr>
<tr><td>400</td><td>Sparta at war with Tissaphernes: Thibron in command with what is left of the Ten Thousand (7).</td></tr>
<tr><td>399</td><td>Death of Socrates (2). Dercyllidas takes over the command in Asia Minor (7).</td></tr>
<tr><td>396</td><td>Agesilaus takes over the command in Asia Minor (7). Conon persuades Rhodes to revolt from Sparta (9).</td></tr>
</table>

Dates

395	Death of Lysander. Timocrates sent by the Persian King to bribe Greece to war with Sparta (9).
394	Battle of Cnidus. Conon rebuilds the walls of Athens. Agesilaus leaves Asia Minor (7 and 9).
392	Embassy of Antalcidas (9). Death of Conon? (9).
390	Iphicrates' light-armed peltasts defeat the Spartans (5 and 13).
386	The King's Peace or Peace of Antalcidas (9).
385–3	Artaxerxes' war with Egypt (13).
384	Birth of Aristotle and Demosthenes (6 and 9).
c. 382	Birth of Philip of Macedon.
380	The *Panegyricus* of Isocrates.
378	Nectanebo I begins the last dynasty of native Egyptian kings.
377	Second Athenian League formed.
376	Chabrias victory for Athens off Naxos (2).
374	Persia, with Pharnabazus and Iphicrates, fails in the invasion of Egypt.
370	Death of Jason of Pherae (13).
367	Death of Dionysius I of Sicily (13).
367	Aristotle joins Plato's Academy. Plato visits Sicily.
c. 366	Revolt of the Satraps against Persia (13). Cos founds its new city (6). Eudoxus of Cnidus (7).
c. 360	Persian King's authority re-established (13).
c. 360	Praxiteles flourishing (7).
359	Philip regent of Macedon.
357	Chios, Rhodes, Byzantium and Cos revolt from the Athenian League. Defeat and death of Chabrias (2).
356	Birth of Alexander. Revolt of Artabazus in Asia Minor: helped by Chares the Atherian, and Memnon the Rhodian (13).
355	Athens recognizes the independence of the four cities. Isocrates on the *Peace*.
c. 355	Death of Xenophon.
353	Demosthenes: *For the freedom of the Rhodians*. Death of Mausolus of Caria (6).
351	Artaxerxes' unsuccessful invasion of Egypt. Demosthenes' first *Philippic*.
350	Artaxerxes sends help to Thebes. Phocion takes Athenian help to the Persians in Cyprus.

Dates

347	Death of Plato.
346	Demosthenes *On the Peace*. Isocrates' *Philippus*.
345	Revolt and sack of Sidon (13).
343–2	Artaxerxes' appeal to Greece and reconquest of Egypt (13). Aristotle becomes tutor to Alexander.
342–1	Birth of Menander and Epicurus.
338	Battle of Chaeronea and victory of the Macedonian phalanx (13). League of Corinth under Philip (14). Death of Isocrates.
336	Darius III King of Persia. Philip murdered; Accession of Alexander. Elected general of the Greeks.
335	Aristotle settles in Athens.
334	Alexander in Asia Minor. Battle of the Granicus. Democracies set up in Ionia. Sieges of Miletus and Halicarnassus (11). Decision to disband the navy (11). Alexander in Lycia (12).
334–3	Conquest of Lycia, Pamphylia, western Pisidia, Cilicia (11, 12 and 16).
333	Spartan embassy to Darius (9). Battle of Issus.
332	Capture of Tyre and conquest of Egypt.
331	Foundation of Alexandria. Alexander sends his admiral to clear the sea of pirates (5). Battle of Gaugamela.
330	Death of Darius. Demosthenes *On the Crown* (8).
326	Alexander crosses the Indus.
324	Restoration of the Greek exiles (13).
323	Alexander's death at Babylon in June.
322	Death of Aristotle and Demosthenes. Perdiccas invades Pisidia to secure the route across Anatolia (11).
321	His murder in Egypt. First production by Menander.
319	Syria annexed by Ptolemy.
315	Syria occupied by Antigonus.
314	Freedom of Greek cities proclaimed by Antigonus (7). Zeno comes to Athens (16).
314–3	Last Athenian policing of the sea (5).
c. 312	Birth of Theocritus (6).
312	Seleucus establishes himself in Babylon.
310	Ptolemy annexes Cyprus.
c. 309	Birth of Ptolemy II at Cos (6).

Dates

REFERENCES

My facts have been taken from such essential works as *The Cambridge Ancient History*, Cary's and Tarn's and Rostovtzeff's Hellenistic histories, Bevan's *House of Seleucus*, and the Loeb translations of Diodorus Siculus, Xenophon, Thucydides, Plutarch, Polybius, Appian and Livy—all used, gratefully and so generally that the marking of every separate occasion becomes impracticable. But I have given, as in my former *Ionia*, a set of particular references at the end of every chapter, so that anyone who may be interested can follow the quest independently.

The works quoted are given once in full and then abbreviated or referred to by authors only. See bibliography for full titles and authors.

CHAPTER I

Authorities quoted:
F. Beaufort: *Karamania*.
[1] Plutarch: *P. Aemilius*.

CHAPTER 2

Authorities quoted:
Bernard Randolph, *The present State of the Islands in the Archipelago (or Arches)*, p. 46.
Isocrates, *Panegyricus*, 139; *Philip*, 134.
Thucydides, IV, 51; VIII, 5; 24.
Xenophon, *Hellenica*, I, 6, 16 ff; II, 1, 21 ff; II, 2, 3; II, 1, 1.
Diodorus, XIII, 77 ff; 105 ff.

[1] Pausanias, VII, 4, 8 (Quoting from Ion.).
[2] Strabo, X, 4, 19.
[3] Livy, XXXVII, 27, 1.
[4] D. Magie, *Roman Rule in Asia Minor*, 478–9.
[5] W. Heyd, *Le Commerce du Levant*, I, 492–3.
[6] Randolph, 52.
[7] Strabo, XIV, 1, 35.

References

[8] For Chabrias see Diodorus, XV, 29–35; XVI, 7; Plutarch, *Agesilaus*; Xenophon, *Hellenica*, *passim* from book V; Aristotle, *Oeconomica*, II, 26.

[9] *Measure for Measure*, Act III, sc. 1.

[10] Diodorus, XV, 90 (in 361 B.C.).

CHAPTER 3

Authorities quoted:
Xenophon, *Hellenica*, II, 1, 29; 2, 5–7.
Thucydides, VIII, 16–21; 25; 46 ff.
Diodorus, XIII, 68, 4.
Herodotus, IX, 99; III, 48; 60.
Isocrates, *to Demonicus*, I, 26.
Th. Gomperz, *Greek Thinkers*, II, 56; III, 50–55.

[1] Thucydides, III, 32.
[2] Gomperz, I, 121; II, 46; Strabo, XIV, 1, 18.
[3] Diodorus, XII, 27, 2; Thucydides, I, 116.
[4]   ,,   XII, 28, 3; XIII, 54, 7.
[5] Thucydides, VIII, 79.
[6] Strabo, XIV, 1, 14.
[7] W. D. Dinsmoor, *The Architecture of Ancient Greece*, 134–5.
[8] Plato, Epistle VIII (Loeb).
[9] Diodorus, XIII, 73, 3; 74, 3.
[10] Thucydides, VI, 92.

CHAPTER 4

Authorities quoted:
Randolph, 53–7.
Herodotus, VI, 95; I, 70; VII, 99.
Th. Wiegand: Milet, Bd., III, 1: *Der Latmos* (for the monks of Heraclea and founding of Patmos).
Euripides, *Women of Troy* (Everyman tr.).
J. W. Mackail, *Select Epigrams from the Greek Anthology*, 3. XXVIII, Theaetetus.

[1] C. T. Newton, *Travels and Discoveries in the Levant*, II, 235.
[2] Thucydides, I, 13.

References

CHAPTER 5

Authorities quoted:

H. A. Ormerod, *Piracy in the Ancient World*, 13; 115–6; 123; 17; 18;
  19; 100; 62; 26; 25.

Thucydides, III, 33; 3. VIII, *passim*.

Diodorus, XV, 44–XVI, 57, *passim*.

Isocrates, *Panegyricus*, 115.

Herodotus, I, 2.

Beaufort, *Karamania* 114.

Xenophon, *Hellenica*, VI, 2, 27 ff for Iphicrates quotation.

1 Xenophon, *Hellen*, II, 1, 30.
2 Demosthenes, *c. Phor*, 23.
3 Quintus Curtius, *Hist. of Alexander* IV, 8, 15.
4 Randolph, 38 and 33.
5 H. W. Parke, *Greek Mercenary Soldiers*, 55 ff; 74; 127.

CHAPTER 6

Authorities quoted:

Diodorus, XV, 76, 2; XIII, 69, 5; XX, 50, 4.

Strabo, XIV, 2, 19.

G. T. Griffith, *Mercenaries of the Hellenistic World*, 90.

Magie, 102.

Tarn and Griffith, *Hellenistic Civilization*, 112; 255–6; 97; 109.

M. Cary, *History of the Greek World*, 138 and 105; 293; 55; 343–51.

Gomperz, I and IV, *passim*.

W. M. Leake, *Journal of a Tour in Asia Minor*, 226.

Newton, I, 333; II, *passim*.

Beaufort, 105.

1 *Idylls of Theocritus*, (A. Lang tr.); Tarn and Griffith, 276.
2 Herodotus, VII, 99.
3 *Camb. Anc. History* V, 44.
4 Newton, II, 143; Beaufort, 99.
5 Newton, II, 127; Ximenes, *Asia Minor in Ruins*, quoting from Claude
  Guichard, *Funerailles et diverses manières d'ensevelirdes Romanis, Grecs
  et autres nations*; Lyons, 1591.

CHAPTER 7

Authorities quoted:

J. M. Cook: *Cnidia: Ann. Brit. Sch. at Athens*, XLVII, 1952.
  (essential for the ancient topography of Cnidus).

References

Magie, 87; 51; 816; 234–40.

Pausanias, V, 24, 7; X, 11, 3.

Newton, II, 160–71; 193–5; 215–38.

For Tissaphernes, Pharnabazus, and autonomy see: The *Camb. Anc. Hist.*, VI; Thucydides, VIII; Diodorus, XIII and XIV; Xenophon *Hellenica* (and *Anabasis* for Tissaphernes and the Ten Thousand); Plutarch; *Agesilaus; Lysander; Alcibiades.*

Herodotus, III, 138.

Cary, 347; Gomperz, III, 138.

[1] Strabo, XIV, 2, 15.

[2] Pausanias, I, 1, 3.

[3] *Elegy and Iambus* (Loeb. tr.), II, 11; 17.

[4] Beaufort, 82.

[5] Herodotus, I, 144; VII, 153.

[6] Iliad, II, 671.

[7] Thucydides, VIII, 35 ff.

[8]   „   III, 31.

[9]   „   III, 47; VIII, 48; 64.

[10] Dinsmoor, 138.

CHAPTER 8

Authorities quoted:

Newton, II, 259–60; 230.

Herodotus, I, 174.

Demosthenes, *Third Philippic*, 36.

[1] Cook, *Ann. Brit. Sch. at Athens*, XLVII, 1952.

CHAPTER 9

Authorities quoted:

Diodorus, XIII and XIV.

Xenophon, Hellenica, I, 1, 14; II, 1, 5; 12; III, 4, 27; IV, 3, 10–14; V, 1, 13–32.

Thucydides, VIII.

Isocrates, *Philip*, 62; *Panegyricus*, 142

[1] Xenophon, *Hellenica*, IV, 8, 9.

[2] Demosthenes, *Lept.*, 68.

[3]   „   : *On the Crown*, 208 (Everyman trans).

[4] Thucydides, VIII, 18; 36; 57.

[5]   „   VIII, 57; 76.

References

[6] Xenophon, *Hellenica*, V, 1, 31; Diodorus, XIV, 110, 3.

[7] Isocrates: *Peace*, 94.

[8] Thucydides, VIII, 2.

[9] Isocrates: *Panathen.*, 142.

[10]   ,,   *Philip*, 120; 132.

[11] Xenophon, *Hellenica*, III, 5, 1; Plutarch, *Agesilaus*.

[12] Isocrates, *Peace*, 68; *Panegyricus*, 121.

[13] Demosthenes: *On the letter of Philip*, 6

[14] E. R. Bevan: *The House of Seleucus*, II, 99.

[15] Magie, 424.

CHAPTER 10

Authorities quoted:

Fraser & Bean: *Rhodian Peraea and Islands.*

Strabo, XIII, 4, 17; XIV, 2, 5–7.

For the description of Rhodes: *Camb. Anc. History*, VII, 207; VIII, 621 ff.; Griffith, 81; Tarn and Griffith, 176; S. Zervos: *Rhodes*, 212–14; 165–76; Newton, I, 162; 138–53; Magie, 71–2.

[1] Pausanias, III, 19, 9.

[2] Pindar, *Olymp.* VII.

[3] Plutarch, *Cicero*.

[4] Pliny, *Nat. Hist.*, XXXV, 105.

[5] E. Biliotti, *L'Isle de Rhodes*, 35.

[6] Strabo, XIV, 2, 5: note in Bohn trans.

[7] Randolph, 26–7.

[8] Chaucer: *Parliament of Foules.*

[9] Polybius, *Histories.*

[10] Herodotus, I, 172.

CHAPTER 11

Authorities quoted:

Herodotus, I, 172; VIII, 87; I, 78; 84.

[1] T. A. B. Spratt and E. Forbes, *Travels in Lycia, Milyas and the Cibyritis*, XI; Fellows, 451.

[2] Strabo, XIV, 2, 3.

[3] Magie, 50; 816.

[4] Thucydides, VIII, 87.

[5] Arrian: *Anabasis*, I, 20, 1 Loeb tr.; Tarn, *Alexander the Great*, I, 19 and II, App. 5.

[6] Fellows, 186; 287.

References

CHAPTER 12

Authorities quoted:

Herodotus, I, 84; 173–6; IV, 35; VII, 92.

Iliad, XII; IV; V; VI; II.

Fellows, 323; 492; 434; 470 (from Proclus).

[1] Cicero, *De Divin.*, I, 41; Pliny, Nat. Hist. XXX, 2.

[2] Arrian, *Anabasis*, II, 3, 3.

[3]   „   „   I, 25, 7–10; IV, 3, 7.

[4] Herodotus, I, 173; Nich. of Damascus, *F. H. G.*, III, 461.

[5] Bacchylides, *Lyra Graeca* (Loeb), III, 193.

[6] Herodotus, I, 173; Fellows, 413–6 (from Steph. Byzant.).

[7] Pausanias, I, 19, 3.

[8] Heyd, I, 547; Beaufort, 79.

[9] Perrot et Chipiez: *History of Art in Phrygia, Lydia, Caria and Lycia*; Choisy: *Histoire de L'Architecture*, I, 251; Dinsmoor, 67–8; Fellows, 315.

[10] Magie, 522.

[11] Dinsmoor, 123; 145.

[12] Plutarch, *Brutus*, 30–1; Magie, 385–6; 389.

[13] Aristotle, *Oeconomica*, II, 2, 14 (Loeb trans.)

[14] About 410 or 400 B.C. acc. to Dinsmoor, 256.

[15] Arrian, *Anabasis*, I, 24, 4–5.

[16] Magie, 523 ff; Strabo, XIV, 3, 2–3.

[17] M. Rostovtzeff: *Social and Economic History of the Hellenistic World*, 355–8.

CHAPTER 13

Authorities quoted:

Fellows, 166; 346; 333.

Leake, 321.

Pausanias, IX, 41, 1.

Leopardi: La Sera del dì di festa.

Livy, XXXVII, 24, 11 ff.

P. H. Davis: *R. Hort. S. Journal*, March 1949.

Isocrates, *Peace*, 47; *Philip*, 55.

Aristotle, *Polit.*, VI, 1319a.

Parke, 230.

[1] Livy, XXXVII, 15, 6; 17, 10.

References

[2] Strabo, XIV, 3, 6.

[3] Fellows, 360.

[4] Magie, 241-2; 219; Appian, Mithrid, 10, 70.

[5] Plutarch, *Nicias*, 12.

[6]   ,,   *Alexander*, 5.
   For the history of the mercenaries: Herodotus, I, 171; VIII, 26; Parke,
      5; T. R. Glover, *From Pericles to Philip*, 35; Diodorus, IX, 32, 1;
      Thucydides, III, 3; VII, 9; VII, 2; Xenophon, *Anabasis*, VI, 2, 10;
      Hellenica, VII, 1, 23; Griffith, 238.   For Mentor: Diodorus, XVI, 42,
      1-58, 2; Parke, 169.

[7] Parke, 105 from Polyaenus, III, 9, 56.

[8] Diodorus, XVI, 22, 1; Demosthenes, *First Philippic*, 24.

[9] Xenophon, *Hellenica*, VI, 1, 5-6.

[10] Parke, 122; 125.

[11]   ,, 228-9; Griffith, 303, ff; Xenophon, *Hellenica*, V, 2, 21.   Dio-
      dorus, XVIII, 8, 5.

[12] Parke, 232-3.

[13] Aristophanes, *Lysistrata*, 557 ff. (B. B. Rogers' tr.).

[14] Thucydides, III, 49.

[15] Parke, 227; 105; Diodorus, XV, 38, 1.

[16] Diodorus, XVIII, 61, 4; XVI, 44, 4; Parke, 166.

[17] Beaufort, 18.

CHAPTER 14

Authorities quoted:
Fellows, 355; 363.
Charles Texier: *Asie Mineure*, 691 ff.
Strabo, XIV, 3, 7.
Beaufort, 27 ff.

[1] Heyd, I, 96; Texier, 691.

[2] Leake, 320; Dinsmoor, 311-18; Texier, 693.

[3] A. M. H. Jones: *The Greek City*, 245.

[4] Aelius Aristides, Or. XXVI, 97 ff (Keil).

CHAPTER 15

Authorities quoted:
Livy, XXXVII, 23 ff.
Beaufort, 43.

References

Cicero, *Verres*, II, 1, 21, 56.
Magie, 1375.

[1] Adopted son, and heir, to Augustus.   Magie, 481.
[2] Beaufort, 57–8.
[3] Plutarch, *Cimon* 12.
[4]   ,,   *Pericles*.
[5] Thucydides, II, 69.
[6] Xenophon, *Hellenica*, III, 1, 1.
[7] Strabo, XIV, 5, 7; Magie, 1168.

CHAPTER 16

Authorities quoted:
Fellows, 399.
Dr. Smith's *Classical Dictionary*.
For Phaselis: Cicero, *Verres*, II, 4, 10, 22; Livy, XXXVII, 23, 1; Pauly
Wissowa, XIX, 1874; Texier, 698; Herodotus, II, 178.

[1] Texier, 697; Beaufort, 48–51; Newton, I, 345.
[2] Diogenes Laertius, VII, 1, 1–3; Glover, 181 ff.
[3] Pausanias, III, 3, 8.
[4] Arrian, *Anabasis*, I, 20, 1; 18, 6.

BIBLIOGRAPHY

GENERAL WORKS

The Cambridge Ancient History.

Diodorus of Sicily: *The Library of History.* Vols. IV–X Loeb trans.

Xenophon: *Hellenica:* (Loeb trans.).

Thucydides: (Everyman trans.).

Herodotus: (Everyman trans.).

Sir Charles Fellows: *Travels & Researches in Asia Minor:* London, 1852.

C. T. Newton: *Travels and Discoveries in the Levant.* London, 1865.

M. Rostovtzeff: *The Social & Economic History of the Hellenistic World,* Oxford, 2nd ed.

Pauly- Wissowa-Kroll *Real Encyclopaedie d. class. Altertdumdswissenschaft.*

Plato: *Epistles:* (Loeb.)

Euripides: *Plays* (Everyman trans.).

IN THE ORDER OF QUOTATION

F. Beaufort: *Karamania.* London 1818 (2nd ed.)

Plutarch's Lives: (Everyman trans.).

Plato's Dialogues: (Jowett's trans.).

Bernard Randolph: *The present State of the islands in the Archipelago (or Arches) Sea of Constantinople, and Gulph of Smyrna; with the islands of Candia, and Rhodes.* Oxford, 1687.

Isocrates: (Loeb trans.).

Strabo: (Loeb trans.).

Pausanias. (Abbé Gedoyn trans.).

Livy: (Loeb trans.).

David Magie: *Roman Rule in Asia Minor.* Princeton, 1950.

W. Heyd: *Histoire du Commerce du Levant.* Leipzig, 1923.

Aristotle: *Oeconomica:* (Loeb trans.).

Th. Gomperz: *Greek Thinkers,* trans. by L. Maguire. London, 1949.

W. B. Dinsmoor: *The Architecture of Ancient Greece.* London, 1950.

Th. Wiegand: *Milet: Der Latmos.* Berlin, 1913.

Bibliography

J. W. Mackail: *Select Epigrams from the Greek Anthology*. London, 1928.

H. A. Ormerod: *Piracy in the Ancient World*. London, 1924.

Demosthenes: (Loeb trans.).

Quintus Curtius: *History of Alexander:* (Loeb trans.).

H. W. Parke: *Greek Mercenary Soldiers*. Oxford, 1933.

G. T. Griffith: *Mercenaries of the Hellenistic World*. Cambridge, 1935.

Tarn & Griffith: *Hellenistic Civilization*. London, 1952.

M. Cary: *A History of the Greek World*. London, 1951.

W. M. Leake: *Journal of a Tour in Asia Minor*. London, 1824.

Theocritus: *Idylls*, trans. by A. Lang.

Ximenes: *Asia Minor in Ruins*. London, 1925.

J. M. Cook: *Cnidia. Annual of the Brit. School at Athens*, XLVII. 1952.

Elegy and Iambus: (Loeb trans. by J. M. Edmonds).

Iliad: (Lang, Leaf & Myers trans.) 1949.

E. R. Bevan: *The House of Seleucus*. London, 1902.

S. Zervos: *Rhodes*. Paris, 1912.

Pindar: (E. Myers' trans.).

E. Biliotti: *L'Isle de Rhodes*, 1881.

C. Seltman: *Approach to Greek Art*. London, 1948.

Polybius: *Histories:* (Leob trans.).

T. A. B. Spratt and E. Forbes: *Travels in Lycia, Milyas and the Cibyritis*.
  London, 1947.

Arrian: *Anabasis:* (Loeb trans.).

W. W. Tarn: *Alexander the Great*. Cambridge, 1951.

Cicero: (Loeb trans.).

Perrot and Chipiez: *History of Art in Phrygia, Lydia, Caria & Lycia*.
  London, 1892.

Choisy: *Histoire de l'Architecture*. 1899.

Fraser & Bean: *Rhodian Peraea and Islands*. Oxford, 1954.

Appian: (Loeb trans.).

P. H. Davis: *Royal Horticultural Society Journal*. March, 1949.

T. R. Glover: *From Pericles to Philip*. London, 1910.

Aristophanes: *Lysistrata:* (B. B. Rogers' trans.).

Charles Texier: *Asie Mineure*. Paris, 1862.

A. H. M. Jones: *The Greek City*. Oxford, 1940.

Diogenes Laertius: (Loeb trans.).

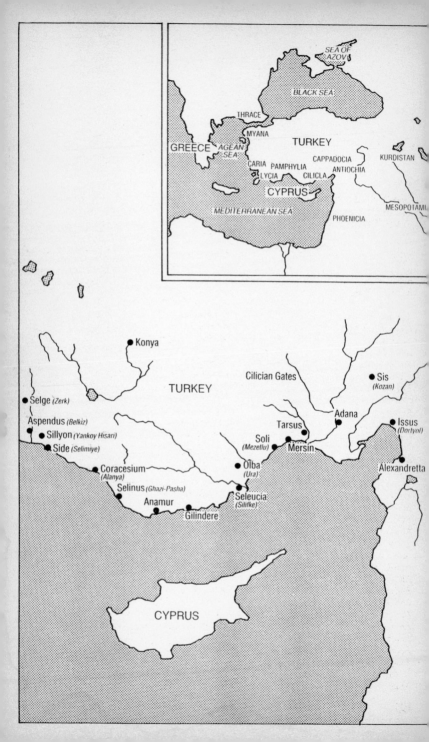

INDEX

Index

Index

Index

Index

Index